中学校英語サポートBOOKS

帯活動で書く力が
ぐんぐん伸びる

3分英作文の指導アイデア

水谷 大輔 著

生徒熱中！
思わず書きたくなる
51の作文テーマ

3分の帯活動＋まとめ20分でできる！
コスパ最強の指導法

明治図書

推薦の言葉

　どなたにもできるライティング指導の方法として，3分英作文をお勧めします。
　中学校でも高校でもライティングは敬遠されがちです。どうやって書かせるのかわからない，書かせた後の添削が面倒だ，などということで，結局はやらないで過ごしてしまうことが多く見受けられます。
　そこで，著者の水谷さんは，誰にでもできる方法を模索して，本書のような3分英作文にたどりつきました。
　生徒は直ぐにはたくさん書けません。第一そんなに授業時間をライティングに当てることが出来ません。
　そこで，毎時間3分だけ，しかも，3分間に1文だけ書けば良い，というやりかたを考案したのです。同じテーマについて，1日目は最初の1文を書き，続きの1文を次の授業に，その続きはそのまた次の授業で書くという仕掛けです。
　これだと生徒に対する負担も少なく，時間を空けて続けるので，生徒にも内容を膨らませるアイディアが徐々に湧いてきます。
　もう1つの大きな問題，「添削問題」をこの方式は見事に解決してくれます。生徒の書く文は1回に1文ですので，40人のクラスでも40個の文を見れば良いことになります。テーマが同じですから，生徒の書く内容も似通っています。授業の合間にサッと目を通してコメントすることができるので，先生方の負担になりません。
　1つだけ今後の課題と言うべきものは，テーマの選択です。水谷さんもこの点，一番苦労されました。本書には51のテーマが挙げられていますが，読者の皆さんも実際に実践してみて，生徒が盛り上がったテーマ，うまく行かなかったテーマなどの情報を交換，共有してゆくと3分英作文という方式が完璧なものになって行くと思います。
　書けるようにするためには書かせ続けなければなりません。生徒への負担も少なく，先生方の添削にも負担がかからない，この方法は汎用性の高い方式だと言ってよいと思います。本書をお読みになった全国の読者の方々が，この方式で生徒の書く力を伸ばしていってほしいと思います。3分英作文を全国の英語の先生に強く推薦いたします。

東京学芸大学名誉教授
金谷　憲

はじめに

「いつの間にかたくさん書けているからびっくりする。」
「回数を重ねるごとに書ける量が増えていくことに驚いた。」
「作文のテーマが面白いからどんどん書ける。」
「他の人の作文を読むのが本当に面白い。」
「他の人に自分の作文を読んだり聞いたりしてもらえるからやる気が出る。」
「模試の英作文の点数がアップした。」

…これらは,「３分英作文」の指導をした生徒からの感想です。

　もし生徒の意欲と能力をより向上させることができるだけでなく,教師の手間をより少なくした英作文指導法があったら,ぜひやってみたいと思いませんか？

　英作文指導,と聞いて,先生方は「時間がかかる」「添削が大変」「書けない生徒への支援が大変」…などなど,あまり英作文指導に対してよい印象を持っていないのではないでしょうか。英作文は生徒にとってはとてもよい活動であることは間違いないのだけれど,教師の負担があまりにも大きい。この辺りはほとんどの先生方が直面するジレンマではないでしょうか。
　「英作文,やりたいけれど,やりたくない。」そんな俳句のような悩みを英語の先生方は誰もが一度は思ったことでしょう。私自身,「今年は英作文指導をがんばるぞ！」と４月に意気込んだものの,いざやってみると思うような効果も上がらないし,何より指導が大変で,途中で挫折してしまったということが何度もありました。先生方も,日常的に英作文指導を取り入れたいと思いつつもその大変さゆえに,一通り文法などを教えた後の「まとめ的活動」「発展的活動」として英作文をスポットで取り入れるだけに留まり（それを否定するわけではなく,もちろんそれだけでも一定の効果はある）,中には「うちの生徒は作文以前にもっと基礎的なことからやらなければならない」と,はじめから作文指導をすることを諦めていらっしゃる方もいるのではないでしょうか。
　作文指導というのは実に難しく,単に白紙だけ与えて「はいどうぞ」と書かせればよいというものではなく,それまでにモデルを提示したり,重要フレーズを教えてあげたりとあれやこれやと下地作りをしてあげたり,適宜支援をしながら書かせていかなければならないということは,先生方もご承知のことだと思います。
　本著を手にしてくださった先生方は,そうした英作文指導の悩みを抱えておられたり,あるいは,いまよりもよい英作文指導法があったら試してみたいとお思いになられたりしている方ではないかと思います。本著で紹介する「３分英作文」の指導は,誰でも今すぐ始めることが

できて，なおかつ，指導や添削がとってもラク。さらに生徒の作文量を大幅に増やすことができるだけでなく，より興味を持って意欲的に活動させることができるものです。

　この「３分英作文」指導では，１回の授業の冒頭３分を使って「一問一答」を繰り返し，それをあとで「まとめ」の時間でまとめさせるという２段階のステップを踏むだけで，どんな生徒にも面白くて長い英作文を書かせることができます。さらに「交流」のステップで，クラスメイトの作品に触れたり，クラスメイトから感想をもらったりして，さらなる意欲につなげることができます。

　実際に「３分英作文」指導をすることで私の受け持った生徒は，費やした時間は従来と同じ50分間であっても，300語に迫る作文を次々と完成させていきました。学習習熟度の低い生徒であっても，何も書けないまま終わってしまうことはありませんでした。しかも，作文の内容も一人一人それぞれの考えや思いが込められた「自己表現」になっています。最後に完成した作文（私は「作品」と呼んでいますが）をクラスメイトたちと共有することで，生徒間で新たな発見をすることができます。「あの人はこんなことを考えていたのか」「あの子はこんなことが好きだったのか」とより深く他者を知ることができ，それで生徒間の関係を温かくすることもできます。英語の技能的にも「こんな表現の仕方があったのか」「こうやって書けば良いのか」といった気づきが生まれ，「早く次を書きたい」と思わせることができます。

　学力的には，この「３分英作文」指導をしている３年生の県学力状況調査において，（具体的な数字は申し上げられませんが）「表現の能力」のポイントが県平均を大幅に上回ったという結果が出ています。

　「３分英作文」のメリットは，こうした生徒側だけにあるわけではありません。教師側の立場になってみても，とても添削が容易にできるというメリットがあります。私は120名程度の生徒を受け持っていますが，全生徒の作文を添削するのに放課後遅くまで追われる，ということはありません。

　このように，「３分英作文」は，生徒に力をつけてあげられる上に，教師の労力がかからないという，とてもコスパのいい指導法です。さらに，こちらが準備するものは何もありません。時間をかけて教材研究をする必要もなければ，凝ったワークシートを作成する必要もありません。ノートを一人一冊用意していただければ，すぐに始めることができます。特別な教授スキルを必要とするものでもありませんので，経験の浅い先生にも指導をすることができます。

　決まった手順を踏むだけで，あとはアレンジ自由です。実際にこの「３分英作文」を授業で試していただき，ご自身で改良を加えながら，よりよいものに育てていってほしいと思います。

2018年６月

水谷　大輔

本書の使い方

テーマについて
テーマについて100～300語程度の英作文をすることが指導の目標になります。テーマは大きく①事実・出来事について書くもの，②想像力・発想力を働かせて書くものに分かれています。

一問一答について
毎授業のはじめに，Qを1つずつ大きく黒板に提示します。少し英語が苦手な生徒でも3分で解答できる内容になっています。

実施おすすめ学年について
どのテーマも，**内容的には**，すべての学年にやらせることができます。（卒業に関するテーマの50と51は除く）

ただし，**文法的には**，最適と思われる学年があります。◎→○→無　の順に適しています。

◎：基本的には手を加えることなくそのまま指導可能。
○：そのまま指導しても問題ないが，その学年・生徒の実態によりフィットするように「一問一答」を少し変更（難しくしたり簡単にしたり，追加したり削除したり）すればよい。

解答例について
一問一答とまとめ作文の解答例です。一問一答をまとめ作文に生かした部分には下線を引いてあります。

プラス1センテンスについて
手が止まってしまった生徒にもう1文プラスで書かせるための声かけの具体例を示しました。生徒の実態に応じてアレンジしていただければと思います。

CONTENTS

推薦の言葉　3
はじめに　4
本書の使い方　6

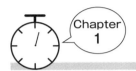

Chapter 1　事前準備なし！今すぐはじめる3分英作文

「3分英作文」指導の流れ　12
STEP1　「一問一答の3分」でネタ作り　14
STEP2　「まとめの20分」で作品完成　16
STEP3　「交流」をして意欲を向上　18
「3分英作文」指導上のギモン　20

Chapter 2　表現力大幅アップ！3分英作文おすすめテーマ

1	1年 2年 3年	Hello! My name is...　自己紹介をしよう	24
2	1年 2年 3年	Introduce a family member　私の家族を紹介します	26
3	1年 2年 3年	My favorite food　私の大好物！	28
4	1年 2年 3年	My treasure　私の宝物	30
5	1年 2年 3年	The thing I want　私が今，欲しいもの	32
6	1年 2年 3年	An alien has come　宇宙人の襲来	34
7	1年 2年 3年	Who is this?　この人は誰でしょう？	36

	学年	タイトル	ページ
8	1年/2年/3年	My dream house 理想の我が家	38
9	1年/2年/3年	A new idol group アイドルをプロデュース	40
10	1年/2年/3年	My smartphone app こんなアプリがあったらいいな	42
11	1年/2年/3年	My movie 目指せアカデミー賞！ 私の初監督映画	44
12	1年/2年/3年	My dream husband/wife 私の白馬の王子様	46
13	1年/2年/3年	A new animal 新種発見！ 新しい動物を考えよう	48
14	1年/2年/3年	New subject in school 新しい教科をつくろう	50
15	1年/2年/3年	A new attraction 遊園地の新アトラクションを考えよう	52
16	1年/2年/3年	A new sport 新しいスポーツ	54
17	1年/2年/3年	A new holiday or festival 新しい祝日	56
18	1年/2年/3年	The food I hate the most この食べ物が大っ嫌い！	58
19	1年/2年/3年	My future self 私の未来予想図	60
20	1年/2年/3年	The country I want to visit 行ってみたいなあの国へ	62
21	1年/2年/3年	The season I like the best いちばん好きな季節	64
22	1年/2年/3年	The best school lunch マイベスト給食	66
23	1年/2年/3年	Who is your hero? 私のヒーロー	68

№	学年	タイトル	ページ
24	1年/2年/3年	I never leave home without… 外出時に必ず持っていくもの	70
25	1年/2年/3年	I don't want to do it! こんなことはやりたくない！	72
26	1年/2年/3年	Format for debate ディベートのお作法	74
27	1年/2年/3年	The bad time 最悪の瞬間	76
28	1年/2年/3年	If you can go back in time… もしもあの時に戻れたら…？	78
29	1年/2年/3年	My school trip 校外学習（修学旅行）の思い出	80
30	1年/2年/3年	Welcome to Japan! 外国人の友達をお・も・て・な・し！	82
31	1年/2年/3年	A useful machine 新しい家電製品を発明しよう！	84
32	1年/2年/3年	To be an animal 動物に変身！	86
33	1年/2年/3年	Another life もしもアニメやマンガの世界に入ったら…？	88
34	1年/2年/3年	Wish comes true もしも魔法のランプがあったら…？	90
35	1年/2年/3年	My superpower もしも私がスーパーヒーローだったら…？	92
36	1年/2年/3年	Alone on an island もしも無人島にひとりでいるならば…？	94
37	1年/2年/3年	Win the lottery もしも宝くじがあたったら…？	96
38	1年/2年/3年	If you are a teacher… もしもあなたが先生になったら…？	98
39	1年/2年/3年	My final day 地球最後の日	100

#	学年	タイトル	ページ
40	1年 2年 3年	100 years in the future 100年後の世界はどんなだろう？	102
41	1年 2年 3年	A person from the past 歴史上の偉人がやってくるヤァ！ヤァ！ヤァ！	104
42	1年 2年 3年	The final meal 最後の晩餐	106
43	1年 2年 3年	The perfect world 理想の世界	108
44	1年 2年 3年	The perfect school 理想の学校	110
45	1年 2年 3年	Interview with a celebrity セレブに突撃インタビュー！	112
46	1年 2年 3年	Three new school rules ３つの新しい校則	114
47	1年 2年 3年	Planning a school trip 楽しい修学旅行計画	116
48	1年 2年 3年	What is the most important for you to do? コレをするのは超大切です	118
49	1年 2年 3年	My Youtube channel チャンネル登録よろしく！私の動画チャンネル	120
50	1年 2年 3年	Three years of memories ３年間の思ひ出ぽろぽろ	122
51	1年 2年 3年	My graduation 卒業～きっと忘れない～	124

おわりに　126

Chapter 1

事前準備なし！今すぐはじめる3分英作文

「3分英作文」指導の流れ

「3分英作文」は，50分を（3分×n回）+（20分）に分けて行う英作文指導法です。
　n＝10とすれば，（3分×10回）+（20分）＝50分になるので，費やしている時間は実質1コマ分になりますが，1コマ50分丸ごと使って英作文させるよりも，作文量が飛躍的に伸びるという魔法の（？）英作文指導です。大きく分けて3つのステップに分かれます。

```
STEP1「一問一答」    3分×n回。一問一答形式の英作文を繰り返してネタを増やす。
STEP2「まとめ」      20分程度。書きためたネタを元に長文をまとめる。
STEP3「交流」        時間は自由に設定。完成した作文を使って生徒間交流をする。
```

STEP1　1回3分の帯活動で「一問一答」をしよう！

「3分英作文」では，まず「一問一答」を毎回3分の「帯活動」として行います。やり方は簡単です。あるお題（テーマ）に沿った質問を1回につき1つ出して，答えさせるだけです。
　※詳しくは，14ページの「STEP1「一問一答の3分」でネタ作り」をご覧ください。

STEP2　「まとめ」の20分を使って作品を完成させよう！

次に，STEP1で書きためたものを「ネタ」として，20分程度の「まとめ」の時間で一気にひとつの長編を完成させていきます。レイアウトは自由。絵を描いてもいいんです。
　※詳しくは，16ページの「STEP2「まとめの20分」で作品完成」をご覧ください。

STEP3　完成した作品で生徒間の「交流」をしよう！

最後に，クラスメイト同士で交換して読みあって感想を書かせたり，壁に掲示したり，あるいはスピーチをさせるなどして交流をしましょう。「交流」を通して自分の考えを伝えたり，人の考えを知ったりする，この活動こそが自己表現活動の醍醐味なんです。
　※詳しくは，18ページの「STEP3「交流」をして意欲を向上」をご覧ください。

STEP1 「一問一答の３分」でネタ作り

```
1. ノートの見開き２ページを使用します。
2. １回３分の「帯活動」で一問一答をして，「ネタ」をためていきます。
3. 毎回ノートを回収して添削をします。
```

「３分英作文」では，まずSTEP1として「一問一答」を毎回３分の「帯活動」として行います。「帯活動」とは，毎回の授業の冒頭で数分を使用して行うルーティーン活動のことです。

このSTEP1「一問一答」のやり方は簡単です。授業者が英語の質問を１つ板書し，生徒がその質問をノートに写し，その下にそれに対する答えを書きます。こう言ってしまえば本当に簡単なのですが，毎回の質問の出し方にちょっとした「仕掛け」があるのです。

例として「自己紹介」をテーマに作文させるとしましょう。最初の帯活動ではQ1として"What is your name?"，次の授業ではQ2"How old are you?"，そのまた次の授業ではQ3 "Where are you from?" と出題します。これに生徒が答えると，A1 "I'm Kawai Yoko."，A2 "I'm 13 years old."，A3 "I'm from Tokyo." といったものになるでしょうか。この３つの答えをご覧になればおわかりでしょうか。このA1からA3の３つの答えをつなげるだけで，もうすでに簡単な自己紹介文が完成しているのです。これが「仕掛け」です。

こちらで意図的な質問を続けることで，特定のテーマに沿った作文が完成するように生徒を知らず知らずのうちに誘導しているのです。質問に対して答えた英文を「ネタ」と呼んでいますが，このSTEP1「一問一答」の目的は，あるテーマに沿った長文を書くための「ネタ」をストックしていくことなのです。

書き終わったら（３分経ったら）ノートを回収して，あとで添削をします。毎回添削をするので，次回生徒の手にノートが渡るときには，前回の作文が添削された状態になっています。生徒は前回自分が書いた英文がどう添削されたかを毎回確かめることができます。

この「一問一答」の添削は毎回行いますが，非常にラクです。というのも，この方式では生徒全員に同じ質問をしているので，生徒全員が同じように答えてくれるからです。自己紹介の例でいえば，Q1 "What is your name?" に対しては，ほとんどの生徒が "My name is ○○." もしくは "I'm ○○." と答えてくることでしょう。これならば，100人程度の添削ならば30分以内に終わらせることができます。

こうして「一問一答」と添削を繰り返して「ネタ」がたまったところで，次のステップ「まとめ」に移ります。

一問一答をしてネタ作文をストックしていこう！

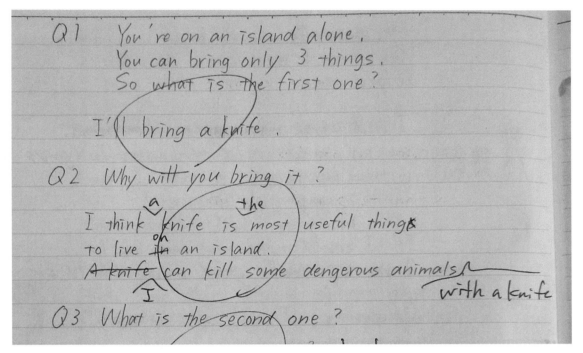

36 もしも無人島にひとりでいるならば……？ 一問一答部分のノート

 指導のコツ！

①意欲的な生徒には「質問に答えるだけでなく，プラスワンセンテンスを書いてみよう。」といった声かけを。逆にスローラーナーには「どうしても英語にできない部分は日本語で書いてくれれば，先生が添削で英語に直しておいてあげるよ。」といった声かけをしてみましょう。

②ノートはページを開いた状態で回収させると，こちらがノートをひとつひとつ開く手間が省けるので，添削がラクになりますよ。

③私はこの活動に入る合図として，3分の某料理番組のテーマ曲，Ken Griffin "Parade of the Wooden Soldiers" を流しています。この曲を流すだけで生徒は条件反射的に「3分英作文ノート」を開いて準備を始めます。

④本書では，Chapter 2で「一問一答集」を51個紹介しています。掲載順に指導する必要はありません。先生方が「面白そう」と思ったテーマから始めてみましょう。

STEP2「まとめの20分」で作品完成

1. ノートは「一問一答」の次ページ（4ページ1組として3ページ目）を使います。
2. 20分で「ネタ」を利用して長編を完成させます。
3. ただ「ネタ」を並べるだけでなく，新たに文を書き足していきます。

　STEP1「一問一答」で「ネタ」がたまったら，いよいよそれをまとめるためSTEP2「まとめ」のステップに入ります。この「まとめ」の時間は，帯活動ではなく，1コマの授業のうち20分程度で設定します。1コマのうち20分を使いますので，残りの30分は通常授業をしてもよいですし，あるいは，次のステップである「交流」をしても構いません。

　この「まとめ」では，一問一答で書きためた「ネタ」を使って長編を作っていきます。接続詞などを用いてネタをつないだり，さらに新たな英文を書き足したりするよう指導しましょう。もちろん，すべてのネタを使用しなくてもよいと付け加えてください。まとめていく過程で不要なネタが出てくることもあるからです。20分程度のこの作業が終わると，ひとつの作品が完成しているという寸法です。

　「一問一答」の段階で添削をしているので，生徒は添削されて正しい英文になっているネタを，安心して「まとめ」で使います。また，生徒に言わせると，まとめているうちにどんどんインスピレーションが湧いてくるらしく，どんどん新しい英文が浮かんできて，書き加えていくことができるそうです。これが「3分英作文」が持っている魔法の力です。いつの間にか，200語を超えるような大作が完成しているのです。絵を描かせたりすると，なお面白いです。私は，レイアウトは自由，絵を描くのも自由，と指導していますので，例えば，マンガ形式で吹き出しに英文を書いたりするなどの工夫が見られました。これも立派な自己表現ですね。

　なお，ノートに「まとめ」をさせるときは，たとえ「一問一答」で使った見開き2ページに十分な余白があったとしても，必ずページをめくって3ページ目にやらせます。そうすることで，まとめているときは「一問一答のページ」と「まとめのページ」をペラペラ何回もめくって行ったり来たりするわけですが，これが地味に効果的です。ネタを見ながら書き写すことができないので，ネタを見ていちど短期記憶に留めてからページをめくって書く，という負荷がかかるからです。これは，ただの音読よりも read & look up のほうが負荷が高いのと同じです。見て，覚えて，めくって，それから書くので，私はこれを flip & write と呼んでいます。

　STEP2「まとめ」が終わったら，最後にSTEP3「交流」です。生徒同士で作品を紹介し合う活動をしましょう。

ノートに自由に表現しよう！

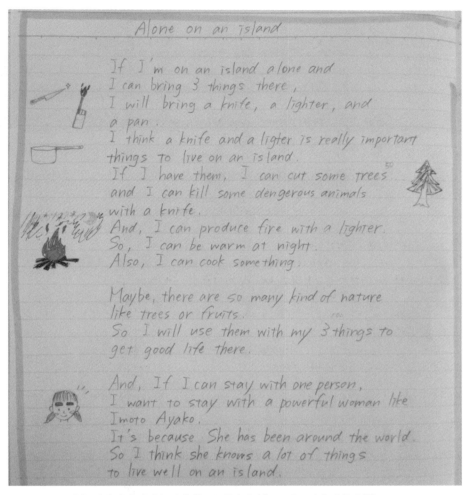

36　もしも無人島にひとりでいるならば……？　まとめ作文例

指導のコツ！

①「まとめ」は静かに取り組ませるよりも，ジャズなどを極々小音量で流してあげたほうが生徒にとっては書きやすいようです。生徒の実態に応じて試してみてください。

②まとめて完成した作品を添削するかどうかは自由です。私は添削をしていません。生徒の創作意欲を削がないようにするためと，生徒の作品に赤ペンを加えるのが申し訳ないような気がするからです。

STEP3 「交流」をして意欲を向上

1. 完成した作品を，生徒同士で紹介し合いましょう。
2. 交流のしかたは様々です。ここでは3つ紹介します。いろいろ試してみましょう。
3. 「鑑賞会」をするならば，まとめのページの右側のページに感想を書かせていきます。

　STEP2「まとめ」を経て完成させた作品を，最後に何らかの形でクラスメイトに発表・紹介させましょう。これをSTEP3「交流」と呼んでいます。相手があってこその自己表現です。人に読んでもらう・聴いてもらうことが表現をする動機づけにつながります。同じ「日本の伝統文化について説明する」という課題であっても「日本の伝統文化について説明文を書きなさい」ではなく「日本に来たばかりのALTに日本の伝統文化について教えてあげよう。書いたらあとでALTに読んでもらいますよ。」とやったほうが，生徒の意欲は増しますよね。

　「3分英作文」でも「交流」を通して仲間に自分の作品が紹介されるからこそ，よりよい作文をして仲間を楽しませたいという気持ちや，よい作文が書けているねと仲間に認めてもらいたい気持ちが働くのです。

　以下に3つの交流の方法を紹介しますが，他にもいろいろな方法があると思います。また，同じ交流方法をずっと続ける必要もありません。あるときはスピーチ，またあるときは掲示，とやってもよいのです。時間的にも生徒の実態的にも適した交流方法を試してみてください。

　①**鑑賞会**…ノートを回して人の作品を読んで，その作品の右ページに感想を書いていくという活動です。回数を重ねると，本書の次ページの写真のようにたくさんの仲間の感想があつまってきます。私は「まとめ」の20分のあと，残り30分でこの「鑑賞会」をすることが多いです。1回3分で作品を鑑賞し感想を書かせます。この方法だと30分で8～9人の作品を鑑賞することができます。1日1作品の鑑賞を3分の帯活動で行わせてもよいでしょう。

　②**スピーチ**…完成した作品を原稿にしたスピーチ活動をするという交流方法です。スピーチにつなげていくために，作品を添削し，音読・暗唱練習をさせる必要がありますが，余裕があれば試したい交流方法です。私がスピーチをするときは，音読・暗唱練習を帯活動で毎回させます。こうすれば，スピーチの練習もしながら通常授業を進めることができます。

　③**掲示**…作品をコピーするなどして掲示するという交流方法です。休み時間などに読ませることができます。交流をする時間が授業で取れないときなどにいかがでしょう。また，英語専用の教室がある学校ならば，その英語教室に掲示させれば教室の雰囲気づくりにもなります。

みんなに読んでもらって感想をもらおう！

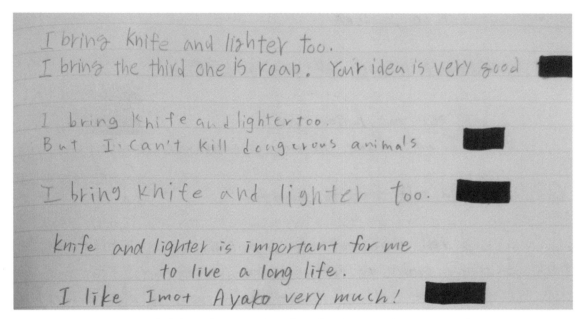

36　もしも無人島にひとりでいるならば……？　クラスメイトからのコメント

 指導のコツ！

①「交流」をすることで，書く活動が他の活動につながっていきます。鑑賞会は「書く」から「読む」（さらに感想を「書く」）活動へ。スピーチは「書く」から「話す（発表）」（さらにスピーチを「聞く」）活動へ。掲示は「書く」から「読む」活動へ。これはどんな技能を鍛える活動なのかと，指導者としては意識しておきたいところです。

②鑑賞会をやっていて気づかされたのは，コミュニケーションは「話す・聞く」だけでなく「書く・読む」によっても成立するのだということ。人の作品を読んで自分の考えや感想を書く活動はまさにコミュニケーションだと思うのです。そういえばSNSも「書く・読む」によるコミュニケーションですよね。

③この「交流」を通じて，クラスの雰囲気がとてもよくなっていくのを私は実感しています。英語を通してお互いの気持ちをわかり合うことができているからです。交流をしているときの生徒の表情はとても穏やかで柔らかい，いい表情です。やっぱり自己表現活動っていいな，と思います。

「3分英作文」指導上のギモン

accuracy が先か？ fluency が先か？

　英作文の指導において，正確性（accuracy。英作文においてはスペリングや文法の正確性でしょうか）を優先させて身につけさせるべきか？　それとも，流暢さ（fluency。英作文においては作文量でしょうか）を優先させて身につけさせるべきか？　もちろん，accuracy も fluency もどちらも身につけさせなければならないものですが，どっちを重点的に伸ばしたほうが，結果的に英語力の伸びが速いのでしょう？

　「3分英作文」の指導者である東京学芸大学名誉教授，金谷憲先生は「fluency が先だ」と断言していました。実際にデータを取ってはいないので感覚レベルの話しかできませんが，私の感覚としても，fluency を意識して指導していれば自然に accuracy も身についてくるものだ，と思っています。というのも，ある文法を習ってからそれを実際に使いこなせるようになるまでには一定の期間がかかるからです。習ってすぐ使えるようにはならないのだから，使いこなせるようになるために間違えながらも，とにかくたくさん書かせていけばいいのだと思います。私だって中学生レベルのミスをすることがあります。だからといって生徒も間違えてよいということにはなりませんが，それだけ完全に習得するには時間がかかるということです。だからたくさん書かせることによって，習ってから身につけるまでの期間を短縮させていくのがよいと思っています。間違ってもいいからとにかく英作文させてみる。多少のミスには目をつぶり，とにかくたくさん書けたことに対して褒めていけばよい。それを繰り返すことでだんだんとミスも減っていきます。

　私は「3分英作文」指導をしていて，「一問一答」では添削をしますが，「まとめ」を経て完成した作品は添削をしません。せっかくがんばってたくさん書いたものに対して赤ペンを入れるのは生徒に対して失礼だと思っているからというのと，あまり赤ペンを入れすぎると，たくさん書く意欲が削がれてしまうこともあるのかな，と思っているからです。

　ではミスの多い作文の評価はどうすればよいのか？　私は，ミスが多いからといって，その生徒の表現の能力が必ずしも低いとは思っていません。ミスが多くても自分のことをうまく表現することができていれば，立派な「表現の能力」だと思うのです。

英作文で誤りを訂正してあげる必要はあるのか？

　英作文指導で先生方の頭を悩ませるもののひとつ，誤りの訂正です。こちらの大変な労力を必要とする割には，生徒は何度も何度も同じ間違いを繰り返す。「前も直してやったのに，また間違えた！」とこぼす先生もいらっしゃるのでは。そもそも誤りを訂正することはフィードバックとして効果的なのでしょうか？

　論より証拠。ここで，金谷憲先生のある研究を紹介します。ある高校の３年生３クラスに対して，同じ英作文の課題を与えました。課題は提出してもしなくてもよいということにし，提出してきたものに対しクラスごとに違うフィードバックをしました。ひとつめのクラス（Ａ組としましょう）は，赤ペンできちんと誤りを訂正して返却する。ふたつめのクラス（Ｂ組）は，赤ペンで誤りの部分に下線を引くだけで訂正はせずに返却する。最後のクラス（Ｃ組）は，添削は何もせずかわいいハンコを押すだけで返却する。さて，数ヶ月このように続けた結果，各クラスの生徒にはどのような変化があったと思いますか？

　まず，英作文の能力ですが，どのクラスも伸び幅は同じだったのです。（なんとＡ組が一番伸びたわけではなかったのです！）次に提出率ですが，Ａ組の提出率はガタ落ちし，Ｂ組は少し下がり，Ｃ組はほとんど提出率が落ちなかったのです。

　もちろん生徒の学力層によっては違った結果が出るかもしれませんが，我々が苦労して一生懸命英作文の誤りを訂正してあげても，それが能力向上には影響を与えないばかりか，生徒の意欲を減退させてしまう可能性もあるということです。

　「accuracy よりも fluency 優先」の理由がここにもあります。前ページでも述べましたが，生徒がある項目を習ってから，実際にそれを自分のものにして，使えるようになるまでには時間がかかるのです。どうも我々教師は，一度教えたらそれですぐに覚えて使えるだろうと思いがちですが，適宜何度も同じ項目を教え直しながら（つまり振り返りをしながら），長い目でじっくりと，身について正しく使えるようになるまで静観するというのが正しいようです。

　ただし，作文したものをスピーチさせるとなると，話は別です。スピーチの際には作成した英文を暗記させますので，間違った英文を暗記させるととんでもないことになってしまいます。スピーチ原稿は誤りをきちんと訂正してあげましょう。

「3分英作文」で入試対策

　入試の英作文問題は，その出題形式は過去の問題から把握できますが，実際に出題されるテーマまでは入試当日までわかりません。入試の英作文問題に対応させるには，生徒に「即興力」をつけてあげる必要があります。

　ここでいう「即興力」とは「その場でいきなり提示された初見のテーマや条件に従って英作文が書ける力」のことです。では，どのような指導をしていけば，初見の英作文課題に対応する即興力をつけてあげることができるのでしょうか。

　私はふたつあると思っています。ひとつは「様々なテーマで何度も練習させておくこと」，もうひとつは「日頃から間違いを恐れずに書かせておくこと」です。

　ひとつめの「様々なテーマで何度も練習させておくこと」ですが，これは言わずもがなだと思います。3年間で一度も英作文をさせてこなかったのに，いきなり入試で作文問題を解けるわけがありません。運動部の部活に例えれば，一度も練習試合をしないで，いきなり本番の大会を迎えさせてもよい結果は生まれませんね。いろいろな学校と練習試合をさせておくことで，どんな相手にも対応できる力が身についてくるというものです。同様に，英作文もたくさん指導しておけばおくほど，生徒の「引き出し」が増えていき，仮に入試で初見のテーマに出会っても「ひょっとしたらあの時のあれが使えるかも」という発想が浮かんでくるかもしれません。

　ふたつめの「間違いを恐れずに書かせていくこと」ですが，これまで述べてきたことにも関連します。私はやはり，日々の英作文指導の中で「間違えずに書くこと」よりも「まず書いてみること」を優先させて指導していくしかないのかな，と思っています。これも運動部の部活で例えてみると，とにかく日頃の練習試合から伸び伸びとミスを恐れずプレイさせておくことです。試合中にミスをするたびにいちいち指導していたら，大会本番ではミスを恐れて思い切ったプレイができません。試合を見ていて部員全員が同じようなミスをするのであれば，後日，そこを練習させればよいのです。話を英作文に戻せば，あまりミスを指摘しすぎると「間違えたくない」という思いが強く働きすぎて，1文目を書けないまま白紙で終わってしまうこともあるかもしれません。ノーミスで終わる試合などめったにないのと同じで，ノーミスで英作文できることもめったにないのですから，ミスを怖がらずに，まず書かせていくのです。何度も書かせていく過程で目立つミスが見つかったら，そこを後日，全体に再び教え直せばいいのです。教え直しをくり返すことで，すこしずつ定着していくのです。1回で100％定着することはないと思って，気長に，指導しましょう。

Chapter 2

表現力大幅アップ！
3分英作文
おすすめテーマ

1 Hello! My name is…

一問一答
3分×9回
まとめ
目安20分

自己紹介をしよう

実施おすすめ学年

1年	2年	3年
◎	○	○

使用する文法事項

be 動詞，一般動詞現在形，日付，動名詞 など

毎回1つずつ，3分間で質問に答えましょう！

1. What is your name?
2. How old are you?
3. Where are you from?
4. When is your birthday?
5. What club (team) are you in (on)?
6. What is your hobby?
7. What are you good at? (What can you do well?)
8. Do you have any brothers or sisters?
9. Do you have any pets?

※未習の文法を含む質問はカットするか，既習文法を用いた同意の質問に作りかえるなどアレンジしてください。

Ⓐ 一問一答の解答例

1. My name is Kimura Saburo.
2. I'm 14 years old.
3. I'm from Miyazaki.
4. My birthday is July 10.
5. I'm on the tennis team.
6. My hobby is watching movies.
7. I'm good at cooking curry and rice.
8. Yes I do. I have 2 brothers.
9. No, I don't. I have no pets.

Ⓐ まとめ英作文の例

　Hello! I am Kimura Saburo. I'm 14 years old. I'm a junior high school student. I'm from Miyazaki. I like chicken nanban very much. My birthday is July 10.

　I'm on the tennis team. I practice it every day. There are 23 members in the team. We are good friends.

　My hobby is watching movies. I watched "Star Wars" last Sunday.

　I'm good at cooking curry and rice. My mother likes my curry!

　I have 2 brothers. Ichiro and Jiro. Ichiro is a doctor, and Jiro is a university student.

　I have no pets, but I like dogs. So I want to have a dog!

⚠ 指導上の留意点

　「3分英作文」をはじめて指導するにあたり，指導の流れを授業者も生徒も双方が理解していく必要がありますが，「あ，こういうことなのね」と理解するためには実際にやってみるのが一番だと思います。そのためにはまず，自己紹介のような「定番」をやるとよいかと思います。この本に掲載する最初のテーマを自己紹介とした理由は，そんなところにあります。ここをスタート地点として，どんどん生徒の発想力に火をつけて，自己表現力を伸ばしていけるようなテーマを採用していってください。

　さて，英語で自己紹介ができるようになるのは，最低限，一般動詞現在形を導入した後になると思います。もちろんbe動詞だけでもある程度の自己紹介はできますが，一般動詞を使った方が，より多くのことがらを説明できるようになります。生徒の学習習熟度，あるいは学年や時期によって，質問を増やしたり減らしたり，あるいはより高度な質問をしたり，もっと面白い質問をしたりと，先生のさじ加減で質問を変えてみてください。

➕1 センテンス

　Q8，Q9については，「もしYesと答えたら，次に先生はどんな質問をすると思う？」という投げかけから，"How many?" "What?" を引き出し，その答えを書かせることができます。

2. Introduce a family member

一問一答 / 3分×8回 / まとめ / 目安20分

私の家族を紹介します

実施おすすめ学年

1年	2年	3年
◎	○	○

使用する文法事項

be 動詞, 一般動詞現在形, 三人称単数現在, want to ～, want 人 to ～
など

毎回1つずつ，3分間で質問に答えましょう！

1. What is his/her name?
2. How old is he/she?
3. What does he/she do?
4. Where does he/she live?
5. What is his/her hobby?
6. What do you like about him/her?
7. What do you want to do with him/her?
8. What do you want him/her to do/be?

※未習の文法を含む質問はカットするか，既習文法を用いた同意の質問に作りかえるなどアレンジしてください。

Ⓐ 一問一答の解答例

1. My brother is Tadashi.
2. He is 19 years old.
3. He is a student.
4. He lives with me and my family.
5. He likes to play sports a lot.
6. He is very cool and kind.
7. I want to introduce him to my friends.
8. I want him to be nice and friendly forever.

Ⓐ まとめ英作文の例

　My brother is Tadashi. I call him Tada. He is 19 years old and he is a student. He is studying very hard. Sometimes, I study with him and he helps me with my homework after school. He is smarter than me. He lives with me and my family. We love him very much. He likes to play sports a lot. He plays soccer and baseball. He likes to swim too. So, he has a good body and is very strong.

　He is not tall, but he has good muscles. He is not very handsome, but he is very cool and kind! He is helpful to others and he likes to talk. He plays sports with me sometimes. I want to introduce him to my friends. I think they will like him very much. I want him to be nice and friendly forever. He is the greatest person in the world.

⚠ 指導上の留意点

　「3分英作文」は，読んだり聞いたりして楽しめるテーマにすると成功する，というのがあります。「他人のこんなこと・こんな考えを知っても…」というテーマでやらせても，なかなかうまくいかないかもしれません。

　ただし，あまり知らない情報について書かせたり，あるいは，楽しめるテーマで書かせたりすると，難しい表現や単語を使わせなければならない場面が出てきてしまう。そこが指導者としてジレンマを感じることだと思います。

　そこで，家族紹介というのはいかがでしょうか。親しい友人の家族のことであれば，知っていることもあるかもしれませんが，あまり話したことのないクラスメイトや，異性のクラスメイトの家族についてはあまり知らないというのが普通のことだと思います。

　人の家族についての英作文はベタなテーマではありますが案外生徒は面白がります。「交流」の時間での感想からは，「この人のお父さんはお医者さんなんだ！」「お母さん，料理上手なんだ！羨ましい…」といった感想がきっと出てくることでしょう。それが他者理解につながり，クラスの雰囲気を温かくすることにつながっていきます。

➕1 センテンス

　Q3では，「より詳しく職業や立場について書いてごらん」という指示を出せばプラスワン，プラスツーと書いていけると思います。

3 My favorite food

私の大好物！

実施おすすめ学年

1年	2年	3年
◎	○	○

使用する文法事項

一般動詞現在形，受動態，how to ～，不定詞，think ～
など

毎回1つずつ，3分間で質問に答えましょう！

1. What food do you like the best?
2. Which country is it from?
3. When (how often) do you eat it?
4. How does it taste?
5. What is used to make it?
6. Do you know how to make it?
7. Do you think other people like it too?

※未習の文法を含む質問はカットするか，既習文法を用いた同意の質問に作りかえるなどアレンジしてください。

A 一問一答の解答例

1. I like pizza the best.
2. It is from Italy.
3. I eat it once a week.
4. It tastes very good!
5. It is made with bread, tomato, cheese, and many more.
6. I don't know how to make it. I want to learn it.
7. Everybody likes pizza!

A まとめ英作文の例

　I like Italian food. I like pasta but pizza is the best of all Italian dishes. Pizza is popular in Japan. <u>I eat it once a week.</u> I usually have it on my birthday. Sometimes I eat it at parties. If there are no parties, I buy one from the supermarket. It is the most delicious food! Eating it makes me happy. <u>It is made with bread, tomato, cheese, and many more.</u> They are sold at pizza restaurants.

　My favorite pizza is the pizza from ABC supermarket. It is not expensive and it is very delicious. It is very big too! It is the biggest of all pizzas in Japan. <u>I don't know how to make it, but I want to learn it.</u> I will make pizza often. I will go to Italy and New York to eat pizza there. Pizza is the best food. <u>Everybody likes pizza!</u>

⚠ 指導上の留意点

　これも「３分英作文」の入門編として，平易なテーマです。一問一答の質問を簡単なものにすれば１年生から書くことができますし，逆に３年生に向けて高度な文法を使用した質問をすることもできます。

　テーマとしてはありきたりなものですが，「好きな食べ物について作文しなさい」という指示を出すだけの，従来の作文指導方法では引き出せないような生徒の考えや思いを，一問一答を工夫することで引き出すことができれば成功だと思います。

　何度も触れますが，「３分英作文」の特徴として「先生や生徒の実態に応じてどのようにでもアレンジ可能」というものがあります。ここでは７つの「一問一答例」を掲載しましたが，例えば「お気に入りのレストランは？」「いつから好きになったの？」「１日３食がそれでも平気？」といった質問をしてみても面白いかもしれません。

　筆者は「まとめ」の時間に，生徒に「絵を描いてもいいよ」と伝えています。創作意欲を湧かせるために，まず絵を描かせてから「まとめ」をさせてもよいと思います。

➕１ センテンス

　Q4を詳しく表現させるために，sour, sweet, salty, bitterなどの「味」もそうですが，chewy, crunchyなどの「食感」を表す単語をいくつか先に教えてあげてもよいと思います。

4 My treasure

一問一答
3分×10回
まとめ
目安20分

私の宝物

実施おすすめ学年

1年	2年	3年
◎	○	○

使用する文法事項
接続詞 if，一般動詞過去形
など

毎回1つずつ，3分間で質問に答えましょう！

1. What is your treasure?
2. What does it look like?
3. When/where did you get it?
4. How did you get it?
5. Tell a special story about it.
6. Why is it your treasure?
7. What do you do with it?
8. Is it helpful/useful to you?
9. If you sell it, how much is it?
10. What will you do if you don't have it?

※未習の文法を含む質問はカットするか，既習文法を用いた同意の質問に作りかえるなどアレンジしてください。

Ⓐ 一問一答の解答例

1. My watch is my treasure.
2. It is silver and big.
3. At my house on my birthday.
4. My father gave it to me.
5. It is not new. My father was wearing it.
6. It is a very cool watch. I like it.
7. I use the alarm every morning.
8. Yes, it is. I can go to school on time.
9. I think it is 5,000 yen. But I won't sell it!
10. I will work hard and buy one.

Ⓐ まとめ英作文の例

　I have a silver watch. <u>My watch is my treasure.</u> <u>It is silver and big.</u> My father gave it to me at home on my birthday. But it is not a new watch. My father was wearing it for a long time. He always wore it at home and at work. He liked it very much. It is a very cool watch and I really love it! So, getting it made me happy.

　It is very useful to me. <u>I use the alarm every morning</u>, so I can go to school on time. I think it is 5,000 yen. It is expensive so I take care of it. I must not wear it at school, so I wear it at home or outside. If I didn't get it, I would be very sad.

　I will work hard and buy a new one myself someday. Also, I will buy a new watch for my father too. I will give it to him on his birthday!

⚠ 指導上の留意点

　「宝物」を紹介する英作文です。自分が大切にしているものは、いつ手に入れたのか、なぜ好きなのか、といった詳細な情報をよく覚えているものです。そうした宝物にまつわる細かいストーリーを、英語で書かせてみましょう。

　このテーマで英作文をした場合、スピーチ活動に持っていくことが多いです。実際に宝物を学校に持ってこさせ、それを手に持ち、クラスメイトに見せながらスピーチできればよいのですが、実物を持って来させることは校則など様々な制約があってできないと思われますので、生徒に1枚画用紙を与え、宝物の絵を書かせましょう。その絵を提示しながらスピーチをさせるのです。

　"Please look at this picture. This is my treasure." という冒頭でスピーチを始めさせます。"Do you know what it is?" なんていう呼びかけをさせても面白いかもしれません。

➕1 センテンス

　特にQ5がこのテーマの「キモ」となる部分だと思います。例えば、複数の生徒が同じ宝物であっても、その宝物が宝物になるまでの経緯は、生徒それぞれで違うはずです。それを引き出してあげるのがQ5です。机間巡視をしながら、3分でできるだけ詳しく書くように伝えましょう。書き足らない部分は、後で「まとめ」の時間で続きを書けばよいのです。

5 The thing I want

一問一答 3分×7回
まとめ 目安20分

私が今，欲しいもの

実施おすすめ学年

1年	2年	3年
◎	○	○

使用する文法事項

助動詞 can，比較級，接続詞 if など

毎回1つずつ，3分間で質問に答えましょう！

1. What do you want the most?
2. Do other people have it? Who?
3. How did you know about it?
4. Why do you want it?
5. Where can you get it?
6. How can you get it?
7. If you get it, what will you do with it?

※未習の文法を含む質問はカットするか，既習文法を用いた同意の質問に作りかえるなどアレンジしてください。

Ⓐ 一問一答の解答例

1. I want a smartphone the most.
2. My friends and family have it.
3. I always see people have it. Everyone uses it.
4. It is the most convenient thing.
5. I can get it in many shops.
6. It is easy to buy, but it is very expensive.
7. I will use it to play games, watch videos, and talk to my friends and family.

Ⓐ まとめ英作文の例

　I want a smartphone. I want to have an Apple iPhone the most. It is the most popular smartphone in the world. The first smartphone was an iPhone. Some of my friends and my whole family have it. I always see people have it and everyone uses it. It is the most convenient thing! I can get it in many shops. So, it is easy to buy, but it is very expensive. I think a new smartphone is 80,000 yen. But I think an old smartphone is okay for me. It is cheaper.

　I will use it to play games, watch videos, and talk to my friends and family. I can study and read books with my smartphone. I can take pictures and videos, so I will always remember my memories. I need it because my life will be happier! I will write to Santa, "Please give me an iPhone!"

⚠ 指導上の留意点

　簡単に書かせることができる題材として「欲しいもの」はいかがでしょう。本書では51のテーマを紹介していますが，もちろん3年間の指導計画で，その全てのテーマを行うことは難しいと思いますので，どれか先生方が「生徒にやらせてみたい」と思うテーマを選んで，実際に授業で扱っていけばよいと思います。

　「中学生が欲しいもの」というのは，ありきたりなテーマですが案外奥が深く，「スマホ」「ゲーム」「お金」というものから，「平和」「頭のよさ」などといった抽象的なものを欲しがる生徒もいたりします。

　文法的には「一問一答例」でcanを扱っていますが，1年生初期でも問題なく解答していける一問一答になっています。長い英作文を書くことに慣れていない1年生に対して扱うテーマとしては，自己紹介と同じようにこのテーマは適していると思います。

　また，どの学年でも扱いやすい一問一答になっていますので，これも自己紹介と同様に，1年生から3年生まで持ち上がりで同じ学年を担当できたならば，毎年1回このテーマをやってみても面白いかもしれません。

　Q7ではそれを手に入れたら何をするかという質問をしています。具体的にどんなことをするのかということを2文以上で書かせてみましょう。

6 An alien has come

一問一答
3分×14回
まとめ
目安20分

宇宙人の襲来

実施おすすめ学年

1年	2年	3年
◎	○	○

使用する文法事項

一般動詞現在形，一般動詞過去形，未来表現など

毎回1つずつ，3分間で質問に答えましょう！

1. What is your name?
2. Where are you from?
3. How did you come to the Earth?
4. How long did it take to come here?
5. How old are you?
6. Do you have any family?
7. What language do you speak?
8. Do you have any special talent or powers?
9. How do you feel about the Earth?
10. Why did you come to the Earth?
11. Do you want to stay here?
12. How long will you stay?
13. What will you do here?
14. Please give your message to the humans!

※未習の文法を含む質問はカットするか，既習文法を用いた同意の質問に作りかえるなどアレンジしてください。

A 一問一答の解答例

1. My name is Yuchu Jim.
2. I'm from a place called Yuchu.
3. I used a big ship.
4. It took only a day.
5. I'm 123 years old.
6. Yes, I do. I have five mothers and a father.
7. I speak English only.
8. I can learn very quickly.
9. I think the Earth is beautiful.
10. Because I want to see nature.
11. Yes, I do.   12. Forever.
13. I will travel the world.
14. Take care of the Earth!

A まとめ英作文の例

My name is Yuchu Jim. I'm not from Earth. I'm from a place called Yuchu. It is a great place, but it is very far away. I used a big ship to come here. My ship is very fast. It is faster than a plane. So, it took only a day.

I'm 123 years old. I have five mothers and a father. I have a lot of brothers and sisters too. I can only speak English now, but I can learn very quickly. I want to learn more languages. I want to talk to many people. I think the Earth is beautiful.

I want to see nature. I like the Earth's mountains, forests, and oceans. So, I want to stay here forever and travel the world. Humans, please take care of the Earth!

⚠ 指導上の留意点

「地球にやってきた宇宙人」に生徒になりきってもらって「自己紹介」をしてもらうというテーマです。

「自己紹介」は，あくまでも自分のことについて作文するので，そこに想像力は必要ありませんが，今回のテーマでは，自分が宇宙人になりきるわけですから，そこに想像力が必要になってきます。したがって自分のことについて紹介文を書く活動よりも，少し高度なテーマになってきます。

一人一人がそれぞれの想像力を働かせて作文をしていくわけですから，でき上がった作品は，他の生徒には作成できない完全にオリジナルの宇宙人となります。そこが生徒の創作意欲を刺激するのです。

このテーマの「交流」の仕方としてお勧めしたいのは，ペアを組ませて，ニュースキャスター役と宇宙人役になってインタビュー形式で一問一答のスピーキング活動をすることです。その準備として，一人一人に画用紙を与えて，宇宙人のお面を作らせるとよりリアルで面白いですよ。

プラス1 センテンス

Q10では，なぜ地球に来たのかを尋ねています。何をするのか，いつするのか，どこでするのか，などを詳しく2文以上で書き加えるように伝えてみましょう。

7 Who is this?

一問一答
3分×9回
まとめ
目安20分

この人は誰でしょう？

実施おすすめ学年

1年	2年	3年
◎	○	○

使用する文法事項

三人称単数現在
など

毎回1つずつ，3分間で質問に答えましょう！

1. What is his/her name?
2. What is his/her nickname?
3. Where is he/she from?
4. What language does he/she speak?
5. How old is he/she?
6. What is his/her favorite food?
7. What sport does he/she play?
8. What subject does he/she like?
9. Does he/she have any brothers or sisters?

※未習の文法を含む質問はカットするか，既習文法を用いた同意の質問に作りかえるなどアレンジしてください。

Ⓐ 一問一答の解答例

1. She is Ueda Tomoe.
2. I call her Tomo-chan.
3. She is from Iruma.
4. She speaks Japanese and a little English.
5. She is 14 years old.
6. Her favorite food is pizza.
7. She plays basketball.
8. She likes P.E. and Japanese.
9. She has a little brother, Hikaru.

Ⓐ まとめ英作文の例

　This is my friend, Ueda Tomoe. I usually call her Tomo-chan. She is cute and very friendly to me. So, I like her very much.

　She lives in Iruma. But her house is far away from my house. She studies at my school. We are in the same class together too. We are classmates.

　She speaks Japanese and a little English. But I speak English better than her. Sometimes, I teach her English. We usually do our homework together after school.

　She is 14 years old. I'm as old as her. But her birthday is next month, so she will be 15 years old then.

　Her favorite food is pizza. But pizza is expensive, so she doesn't eat it often. She plays basketball and she is in the basketball club. She likes to study P.E. and Japanese very much. She has a little brother, Hikaru. He is cute. I like him too!

⚠ 指導上の留意点

　このテーマは,「家族紹介・他人紹介」の応用編です。他人紹介では,実在のクラスメイトや家族を紹介しますが,このテーマでは,こちらで人物を提示して,それがどんな人物であるかを創作させるという活動です。

　提示する人物は,生徒全員が知らない・見たことのない人物の方が,創作意欲が出てくると思います。たとえば有名人を提示してしまうと,その人を知っているか知らないかでハンデがありますし,また,創作活動ですので,知っている人物を提示してしまうと,どうしてもその人物本来の職業や名前にとらわれてしまい,自由な発想ができなくなります。少し奇抜な格好をした人物や,一風変わった印象の人物などを描いて生徒に "Who is this?" と提示してみてはいかがでしょうか。

　文法的には「他人紹介」と同様に3人称が主です。したがって,1年生に対してこの活動をやることをオススメします。写真や絵を変えれば,何度も何度も同じ活動をすることができます。

➕1 センテンス

　Q5の後に What is his/her job? のような質問をすると,よりその人の人物像が色濃く出てくるかと思います。とにかく1枚の絵(写真)から,生徒の想像力をどんどん引き出すような質問を投げかけてみましょう。

8 My dream house

一問一答
3分×8回
まとめ
目安20分

理想の我が家

実施おすすめ学年

1年	2年	3年
◎	○	○

使用する文法事項
be 動詞，一般動詞現在形
など

毎回1つずつ，3分間で質問に答えましょう！

1. Where do you want to live?
2. Why do you want to live there?
3. What is the style of your house?
4. How big is your house?
5. How many rooms are there?
6. What is the best room in the house?
7. Tell us about the other rooms.
8. How much is it?

※未習の文法を含む質問はカットするか，既習文法を用いた同意の質問に作りかえるなどアレンジしてください。

Ⓐ 一問一答の解答例

1. I want to live in Tokyo.
2. It is a convenient place to live.
3. My house is in a tall building. I will live at the top.
4. It is big and it has many floors.
5. There are about ten rooms.
6. The best room is the gaming room.
7. There is a pool in the bathroom. The bedroom is the biggest room of all.
8. It is about fifty million yen.

Ⓐ まとめ英作文の例

For my dream house, I want to live in Tokyo. It is the biggest city in Japan. There are so many things to see there. Tokyo city is a convenient place to live. You don't have to go anywhere.

My house in Tokyo is inside a tall building. I want to live at the top of it. I like to see a beautiful view every day. My window has a great scene outside.

It is a big house and it has many floors. I think it has about three or four floors. The house has many rooms. It has about ten big rooms but the best room is the gaming room. My computer and gaming systems are in that room. It also has a big TV. I can stay there for a long time. There is a pool in the bathroom and I swim there. But the bedroom is the biggest room of all. The house is about fifty million yen.

⚠ 指導上の留意点

自分の理想の家を考えてみましょう，というのがこのテーマです。

まず，どこに住みたいか？（Q1）というのは悩みどころですね。都心部に住みたいという人もいれば，山間部に住みたいという人もいるでしょう。なぜそこに住みたいのかという理由も書かせてみましょう。（Q2）

次に家のスタイルを書いてもらいます（Q3）なかなか生徒の筆が進まないようであれば，（3分は超えてしまいますが）いくつか家の写真を見せて，その写真を指差しながら英語でその写真の家の説明をしてから書かせてみるといいでしょう。こういう家は英語ではどのように説明すればよいかが，それで生徒に伝わることでしょう。

Q4～Q7では，実際にどんな部屋があるのかというのを説明していきます。ここに生徒の好みがはっきりと出てくると思います。例文ではゲームをするための部屋があるという作文をしてみましたが，実際に生徒は「ボウリングができる部屋」「バッティング練習ができる部屋」「猫が100匹いる部屋」といったユニークな部屋を書いていました。

「まとめ」の活動では，作文をまとめるだけでなく，家の設計図も描かせてみるといいでしょう。

➕1 センテンス

Q6では Why is it the best room? のような質問をすることで，プラスワンセンテンスを引き出すことができます。

9 A new idol group

アイドルをプロデュース

一問一答
3分×8回
まとめ
目安20分

実施おすすめ学年

1年	2年	3年
◎	○	○

使用する文法事項

be 動詞，一般動詞現在形，How many ～ など

毎回1つずつ，3分間で質問に答えましょう！

1. What is the name of the new idol group?
2. How many members does it have?
3. Who are the members of the group?
4. How old are they?
5. What is their fashion style?
6. What is the group famous for?
7. What else can they do?
8. Who are their fans?

※未習の文法を含む質問はカットするか，既習文法を用いた同意の質問に作りかえるなどアレンジしてください。

A 一問一答の解答例

1. It is called ABC123.
2. There are three boys and three girls.
3. They are Eiji, Billy, Cindy, Wanda, Tommy, and Suri.
4. They are about twenty years old.
5. They wear colorful clothes. They have different colors.
6. ABC123 is famous for their fun songs and dances.
7. They are also in movies and commercials on TV.
8. Young people.

A まとめ英作文の例

The new idol group is called ABC 123. It is a very popular group in Japan. The group has six members. There are three boys and three girls. They are handsome and beautiful people. Their names are Eiji, Billy, Cindy, Wanda, Tommy, and Suri. They are young people from around the world. They are about twenty years old.

They wear colorful clothes and they have different colors. The group is known for their fun songs and dances. They have many songs and they are big hits! You can hear their songs on the radio. They dance very well too. People practice their dance styles.

They are also in movies and commercials on TV. You can see them every day. Their fans are usually young people. I love ABC 123!

⚠ 指導上の留意点

新しいアイドルグループを考えて，プロデュースしてみましょう，というテーマです。

男性，女性ともに，日本にはアイドルグループはたくさんいます。日本という国の音楽シーンの一つの特徴とも言えます。ほとんどの中学生にも好きなアイドルグループがいて，憧れを抱いたり，歌を歌ったりしていますね。ここでは，自分がプロデューサーになったつもりで，新しいアイドルグループを作ってみましょう，ということです。

まずはQ1～4で，グループ名，人数構成，メンバーの名前，年齢，といったプロフィールを書いていきます。

次に服装を決めていきます。それぞれが違った色の服を着てもよいですし，グループのコンセプトカラーを一つ決めて，全員がその色の服を着てもよいでしょう。

そのグループについて何が有名なのか，何が上手なのかというセールスポイントは欠かせません（Q6）。ダンスがうまい，歌がうまい，あるいは，ある特定のスポーツがうまい，といった特徴を書かせてください。メンバー一人一人が違った特技を持っていても面白いかもしれませんね。

➕1 センテンス

Q6とQ7は続いていますが，発想力を働かせて2文以上書かせてみたいところです。生徒が書いた答えを見ながら，What song? や What movie? のような付加的な質問をしてみましょう。

10 My smartphone app

一問一答
3分×8回
まとめ
目安20分

こんなアプリがあったらいいな

実施おすすめ学年

1年	2年	3年
◎	○	○

使用する文法事項

be 動詞, 一般動詞現在形, How much ～ など

毎回1つずつ, 3分間で質問に答えましょう!

1. What is the name of your app?
2. What is the logo design?
3. How much is it?
4. What does it do?
5. What else can it do?
6. How do you use it?
7. When do you use it?
8. Why is it useful?

※未習の文法を含む質問はカットするか, 既習文法を用いた同意の質問に作りかえるなどアレンジしてください。

Ⓐ 一問一答の解答例

1. It is called "Wake Up!"
2. It is a smiling clock.
3. It is free!
4. It is an alarm that won't stop. You have to get out of the room. It will wake you.
5. It will also tell you important schedules.
6. Put in the time to wake up. It is very easy.
7. I use it every morning.
8. It will help people who are late.

Ⓐ まとめ英作文の例

　I love smartphones. It is the most useful thing in the world. There are so many great apps but I want to make my app. <u>It is called "Wake Up!"</u> and it is very useful.

　The logo design is a <u>smiling clock</u>. It is blue and cool. It is great because my app <u>is free</u>. Anyone can download it.

　<u>It is an alarm that won't stop</u>. When you hear it, <u>you have to get out of the room</u>. You have to bring your phone. Then, it will stop. <u>It will wake you!</u> It can <u>also tell you important schedules</u>. You will remember important things. It will help you!

　It is very easy to use. Put in the alarm time or schedule in the app. You can choose the music too. If you choose a very loud music, you will wake up easier. <u>I use it every morning</u> to go to school. <u>It will help people who are always late</u>.

⚠ 指導上の留意点

　新しいスマートフォンのアプリを考えてみましょう，というのがこのテーマです。

　スマートフォンは，（中学生に必要かどうかという議論はここではしませんが）とても便利なものです。スマートフォンの普及により，私たちの生活はとても便利で快適なものになったということは疑いようのないことです。そこで，こんなアプリがあったらいいな，というものを中学生に英語で書いてもらいましょう。

　例文では，自分がなかなか朝起きられないから，部屋を出るまでアラームが止まらないようになっている目覚まし時計アプリを例として書いてみました。このように，完全に「自分専用」の，もしこんなアプリがあったら自分は助かる，というものでもよいですし，世界中の人にとって便利なアプリを考えてもよいです。

　このテーマの「一問一答」はどれも平易で，難しい文法を使っておりませんので，疑問文を一通り学習し終えたならば，1年生でもすぐに取りかかれるテーマだと思います。内容としても中学生の興味をそそり，「書いてみたい！」と思わせられるようなテーマだと思います。

➕1 センテンス

　Q4で実際にどんなアプリなのかを説明していきます。楽しく，便利なアプリの内容を詳しく書けるよう，And then?（それで？・それから？）と投げかけていきましょう。

11 My movie

一問一答
3分×9回
まとめ
目安20分

目指せアカデミー賞！　私の初監督映画

実施おすすめ学年

1年	2年	3年
◎	○	○

使用する文法事項

be 動詞，一般動詞現在形，How long ～，How much ～
など

毎回1つずつ，3分間で質問に答えましょう！

1. What is the title of the movie?
2. What is it about?
3. How long is the movie?
4. Who are the main characters?
5. Who are their actors?
6. Tell us one scene in the movie.
7. How do you feel if you watch it?
8. How much is the ticket price?
9. When is the opening day?

※未習の文法を含む質問はカットするか，既習文法を用いた同意の質問に作りかえるなどアレンジしてください。

A 一問一答の解答例

1. Again, Baby.
2. It is about a man who is a baby again.
3. About two hours.
4. The baby, his parents, and his friends.
5. The baby and his friend are new actors.
6. The baby is talking to adults. He is using LINE. It's funny.
7. It is a very funny and happy movie. I feel great!
8. It is 1000 yen for everyone.
9. It is on December 23rd.

A まとめ英作文の例

My movie's title is "Again, Baby". It is movie about a man who is a baby again. The man was a normal human, but he becomes a baby. He must live a baby's life. It is magic! It is very interesting and funny. You will laugh when you watch it.

It is about two hours. The characters are the baby, his parents, and his friends. His friends are babies too. The baby and his friend are new actors.

There is a funny scene there. The baby is talking to adults and he is using LINE. The adults don't know that the baby was a man. Everyone thinks he is a smart baby. It is a very funny and happy movie. I feel great watching it!

The ticket is 1000 yen for everyone. It is on December 23rd. Please watch it!

⚠ 指導上の留意点

自分が映画監督になったら，どんな映画を作りますか？　というテーマです。

想像力を働かせる，という観点で言えば，映画こそ想像力の宝庫です。日常ではあり得ないような設定やストーリー展開は，映画ならではのことです。目の覚めるようなアクション映画，壮大なSF，感動的なラブストーリー…。あるいは，アニメ映画でもいいです。生徒には，実際に映画監督になって，自分がこれから作る映画の内容を英語で説明してもらいましょう。

まずはタイトルを決めなければなりません。ストーリーが伝わりやすいタイトルを考えましょう。次に，どんな内容の映画かを書きます。

キャストも決めなければなりません。あくまでも想像ですので，好きな俳優，人気の女優を選んでも構いません。もちろん，自分を主演にしてもいいですね。

Q6では実際に映画のハイライトシーンを書きます。どんな映画なのかが一読してわかるように，上手に説明して欲しいところです。

文法的には平易な内容ばかりを扱っていますが，ある程度，語彙力がある3年生の方が面白いと感じるテーマかもしれません。

➕1 センテンス

Q2の映画の内容を，うまく説明してもらうために，適宜効果的な質問を個別に投げかけながら2文以上書いてもらいましょう。

My dream husband/wife

私の白馬の王子様

実施おすすめ学年

1年	2年	3年
◎	○	○

使用する文法事項

look 〜，接続詞 if，未来表現 など

毎回1つずつ，3分間で質問に答えましょう！

1. What is the name and nickname of your dream husband/wife?
2. What does he/she look like? (face, body, hair, height)
3. What is his/her personality?
4. What are his/her job?
5. What will you do on your first date?
6. What present will you give on his/her birthday?
7. What will be your wedding ceremony?
8. Where will you live together?
9. Will you have children or pets?

※未習の文法を含む質問はカットするか，既習文法を用いた同意の質問に作りかえるなどアレンジしてください。

A 一問一答の解答例

1. My wife's name is Mary.
2. She is tall and beautiful.
3. She is kind and smart.
4. She is an ALT.
5. We will go to Hawaii.
6. I will give her our picture together.
7. We will marry at the beach.
8. We will live near the sea.
9. We will have a girl and a boy, and a dog too.

A まとめ英作文の例

My wife's name is Mary. She is tall and beautiful. So, she is like an idol or a model! She is kind and smart too. She likes animals and small children. She can draw beautiful pictures and cook delicious dishes. What a perfect woman! I love her so much.

She is an ALT and I met her at school. She teaches elementary school students. Her English classes are really popular. Everyone loves her.

I think we will go to Hawaii on our first date. She likes swimming. I will give her our picture together as a present. It is a big picture with a gold frame. Then, we will marry at the beach and live near the sea.

I want a big house with a lot of rooms. We will have a girl, a boy, and a dog too! We will be happy forever!

⚠ 指導上の留意点

これは，自分が将来結婚するならばどんな人？　というトピックです。優しい人？　お金持ちの人？　背が高い人？　やっぱりイケメン？　年齢は？　職業は？

自分の理想のタイプを日本語で言い合うのであれば少々恥ずかしいですが，英語で書かせてみると，なぜかどんどん書けてしまうものです。これも英語の魔力でしょうか。

Q1～9の全ての質問は，比較的平易なものなので，どの学年でも取り組ませることができますが，1年生だと少し「照れ」があって筆が進まないかもしれません。少しマセてくる2年生後半から3年生にやらせた方がうまくいくテーマかもしれません。

筆者はよく，3年生の関係代名詞の導入に「理想の結婚相手」を書かせます。

I want to marry a man/woman who …という例文を提示して，同じようにどんどん書かせていくのです。もし，この3文英作文のテーマを3年生後半で扱うのであれば，Q2～4あたりを，関係代名詞を使って書かせるような指示を出しても良いかもしれません。

➕1 センテンス

Q5で，最初のデートについて聞いています。Whatだけではなく，WhereやWhenを用いた質問をし，それにも答えさせることで，最初のデートがより具体的になっていくと思います。

13 A new animal

一問一答
3分×10回
まとめ
目安20分

新種発見！　新しい動物を考えよう

実施おすすめ学年

1年	2年	3年
◎	○	○

使用する文法事項

want to 〜，have to 〜，接続詞 if など

毎回１つずつ，３分間で質問に答えましょう！

1. Please make a new animal. What is the name of the new animal?
2. What does it look like? (face, body, legs, skin)
3. What can it do? (swim, fly, run, jump)
4. What sound does it make?
5. Where does it live?
6. What does it eat?
7. What does it usually do during the day?
8. How about at night?
9. Is it friendly or dangerous?
10. Will it be a good pet?

※未習の文法を含む質問はカットするか，既習文法を用いた同意の質問に作りかえるなどアレンジしてください。

A 一問一答の解答例

1. It is Eaglion.
2. Eaglion has an eagle's face and a lion's body.
3. It can run and fly very fast.
4. It makes a loud shout.
5. It lives in mountains.
6. It eats other animals.
7. It usually sleeps during the day.
8. It finds food at night.
9. It is very dangerous.
10. No, it will fight people!

A まとめ英作文の例

　If I will make a new animal, I will call it an eaglion. An eaglion has an eagle's face and a lion's body. It looks strong and cool. It is big and strong, but it has beautiful colors. It can run very fast. I think it is faster than a cheetah. It can fly too. It flies very high and very fast.

　Sometimes, it makes a loud shout. You can hear it from another mountain. It lives in mountains and forests.

　It lives in tall trees. It eats other animals every day. It likes meat and blood. So, it finds small animals to eat. It usually sleeps during the day, but it finds food at night. The eaglion eyes are powerful and it can see very far.

　It is very dangerous, so it will fight people! Please don't go near it. If you see one, run away very fast. It will catch you!

⚠ 指導上の留意点

　新種の動物を想像してみようというのがこのテーマです。この世の中にはまだまだ不思議なことがいっぱいあって，まだまだ見たことのない動物がいるかもしれません。哺乳類でも鳥類でもない，全く新しい分類の動物がいるかもしれません。少し難しいテーマですが，書かせてみると我々オトナには想像もつかないような面白い動物が出てきて，とても楽しいですよ。

　「まとめ」の時間には，その動物の絵を描かせてみましょう。絵を描くことで，より具体性が増しますし，「鑑賞会」で読み合う時にも，絵があった方が読み進めやすいと思います。

　「3文英作文」の狙いと効果の一つに，創造性を育成するというのがあります。突然与えられたテーマにも柔軟に対応できるように，こういったテーマを与えていくことで，どんな英作文テーマにも対応できるような「即興性」や「対応力」がついてくると思います。自分でストーリーを組み立てる「文章構成力」もついてくると思います。

プラス1センテンス

　Q7，Q8で，この動物の生態を書きます。どんなことをするのか具体的に書かせてみましょう。

14 New subject in school

一問一答
3分×8回
まとめ
目安20分

新しい教科をつくろう

実施おすすめ学年

1年	2年	3年
◎	○	○

使用する文法事項

be 動詞，一般動詞現在形，助動詞 can など

毎回1つずつ，3分間で質問に答えましょう！

1. What do you want to learn?
2. Why is it interesting for you?
3. Please make a new subject in the school. What is the name of the new subject?
4. What can you learn there?
5. What else can you learn there?
6. Why is it a useful class?
7. Who is the teacher?
8. Tell us an example of its homework.

※未習の文法を含む質問はカットするか，既習文法を用いた同意の質問に作りかえるなどアレンジしてください。

Ⓐ 一問一答の解答例

1. I want to learn how to be rich.
2. I want to get money.
3. It is called Money Studies.
4. You can learn how to get money quickly.
5. You can learn how to use it well.
6. Because money is very important in this world.
7. The teacher is Bill Gates.
8. The homework is to plan a business.

Ⓐ まとめ英作文の例

I want to learn how to be rich. It will help me a lot because I want to get money. I want to have a lot of money. Then I will use it every day. If it is a new class in school, it is called Money Studies.

In the class, you can learn how to get money quickly. You will know the secrets. Then it will be easier to get money. You can be rich very fast. Also, you can learn how to use it well. You will get more money. Learning how to get money is important because money is very important in this world. We use it every day for everything. It is the most important thing for us today. It will make us happy.

In this class, the teacher is Bill Gates. He is the richest man in the world. And in this class, the homework is to plan a business. It is difficult but very good!

⚠ 指導上の留意点

中学校で，新しい教科があるとしたら何？というテーマです。

現在，道徳を含めて10教科が中学校には存在しますが，新たな教科を考えてみましょう，という面白いテーマです。

現代社会を生きていく上で，10教科以外にも必要な教科があるかもしれません。筆者は個人的には（自分が経済学部卒だということもあり）おカネについて学ぶ教科があってもよいのではないかと思っています。お金の使い方（運用の仕方）は近年大きく変わってきており，単に貯金をしているだけ，という時代は終わったと個人的には思っています。

それはさておき，生徒に自由に教科を考えさせた時，実に様々な教科を考え出してくれて，とても面白いです。美術の他に「アニメ・漫画」の授業，「ゲーム」など，極めて個人的な好みを教科にしたものから，「心理学」や「韓国語」などといったものを挙げる生徒もいます。何れにしても，Q6で，なぜその教科が有益なのか理由をきちんと述べなければなりません。Q7は特任教授として，講師を招聘するならば誰が適任かを考えさせます。これもまた面白いですよ。

➕1 センテンス

Q6で，それを習うことによって中学生はどう有益なのかを書かせます。時代背景などを踏まえて上手に書かせてみましょう。

15 A new attraction

一問一答
3分×9回
まとめ
目安20分

遊園地の新アトラクションを考えよう

実施おすすめ学年

1年	2年	3年
◎	○	○

使用する文法事項

be動詞, 一般動詞現在形, How long ～, 接続詞 if
など

毎回1つずつ, 3分間で質問に答えましょう！

1. What is your favorite theme park?
2. Why do you like it?
3. What is your favorite attraction there?
4. Please make a new attraction. What is the name of the new attraction?
5. Tell us about the attraction.
6. How do you feel if you ride it?
7. How long does it last?
8. What kinds of people ride it?
9. How long is the waiting time?

※未習の文法を含む質問はカットするか，既習文法を用いた同意の質問に作りかえるなどアレンジしてください。

A 一問一答の解答例

1. It is USJ in Osaka.
2. It is a very fun place to visit. There are many rides.
3. I like the Harry Potter world.
4. The King Kong Gorilla.
5. It is a very exciting ride. It is for adults. You will scream!
6. It will make you scared but it is fun to ride.
7. It takes about five minutes.
8. It is a ride only for adults because it is very scary.
9. Many people want to ride it. So, it takes about two hours.

A まとめ英作文の例

My favorite theme park is USJ. It means Universal Studios Japan. It is in Osaka. It is a very fun place to visit, but it is expensive. There are many rides and attractions. I like the Harry Potter world. I'm a fan of Harry Potter. I have read the books and I have watched the movies too.

I want a new ride. It is called "The King Kong Gorilla". It is a very exciting ride. It is for adults. You will scream! It will make you scared but it is fun to ride. It takes about five minutes. It is a ride only for adults because it is very scary. Many people want to ride it. So, it takes about two hours.

⚠ 指導上の留意点

遊園地の，新しいアトラクションを考えてみましょう，というテーマです。

実際に存在するテーマパーク内に，そのテーマパークのコンセプトに沿ったアトラクションを考えてもよいです。例えば，千葉県の「あの遊園地」で，まだアトラクションになっていないキャラクターを採用して新しいものを考えてみる，というのは面白そうです。もちろん，完全に自分の好みのアトラクションを考えてもよいです。

遊園地が好きな生徒にとっては，どんどん書き進んでいけるテーマだと思いますが，遊園地が嫌いな生徒にとっては難しいテーマかもしれません。そんな時は「遊園地が嫌いな君でも，こんなアトラクションがあったら行ってみたいと思うようなアトラクションを考えてごらん」と伝えましょう。

好きな遊園地がない場合，Q1～3に答えることはできませんので，Q1～3の代わりに，新しい遊園地を1から作らせてみましょう。What kind of theme park do you want to enjoy? だったり，If you can make a new theme park, what kind of theme park do you want to make? といった質問が有効かと思います。（もちろんこの質問を全員にやっても面白いと思います）

➕1 センテンス

Q5がこのテーマの「キモ」です。乗り方（楽しみ方）を，順を追って詳しく書かせてみましょう。

16 A new sport

一問一答
3分×10回
まとめ
目安20分

新しいスポーツ

実施おすすめ学年

1年	2年	3年
◎	○	○

使用する文法事項

want to ~，have to ~，接続詞 if
How many ~，助動詞 can
など

毎回1つずつ，3分間で質問に答えましょう！

1. Please make a new sport. What is the name of the new sport?
2. What are used to play it?
3. Can both men and women play it?
4. How many members in a team?
5. What is the uniform of the players?
6. Which countries play it?
7. What are the rules of the sport? (3-5 rules)
8. How do you win the game?
9. Give an example of a team name.
10. Do you want to play the sport?

※未習の文法を含む質問はカットするか，既習文法を用いた同意の質問に作りかえるなどアレンジしてください。

Ⓐ 一問一答の解答例

1. Basketbell.
2. It uses a normal basketball but the board has a bell on the ring.
3. Yes, they can.
4. It has as many players as normal basketball.
5. The uniform is a large shirt and large shorts.
6. Every country plays it.
7. It is the same as basketball. But if you don't ring the bell, the points are double.
8. Shoot the ball but don't ring the bell.
9. Octo-Bell.
10. Yes, I do.

Ⓐ まとめ英作文の例

　The new sport is Basketbell. This sport uses a normal basketball but the board has a bell on the ring. It rings when you shoot the ball. Men and women can play it. Anyone can play it. It has as many players as normal basketball.

　The uniform is a large shirt and large shorts. They are large and colorful. Every country plays it. The rules are almost the same as normal basketball. You have to put the ball in the ring. When you shoot and hit the bell, it will usually ring. But if you don't ring the bell, the points are double. So, shoot the ball but don't ring the bell.

　Octo-Bell is one of the teams. They are very strong. I want to play it!

⚠ 指導上の留意点

　この世の中にはたくさんのスポーツがありますが，自分たちで新しいスポーツを考えてみよう，というのがこのテーマです。

　既存のスポーツをアレンジして，何か新しいスポーツを作り出してもいいですし，既存のスポーツを複数組み合わせてもいいですし，今までにない全く新しいスポーツを生み出しても構いません。とにかく，生徒たちの自由な発想で，新しい競技を生み出していきましょう。

　まずは名前を決めなければなりません（Q1）。誰にでも覚えやすいような，シンプルな名前を考えさせましょう。Q2～Q5は，実際のそのスポーツの規定に関する作文です。人数や道具，服装について書かせましょう。

　いよいよQ7ではルールを書きます。ここは時間がかかる部分なので，この質問で5回，6回と「一問一答」を繰り返してもいいと思いますし，「まとめ」の時間でじっくりと肉付けさせてもいいと思います。

＋プラス1 センテンス

　Q10ではそのスポーツを実際にやってみたいかどうかを尋ねますが，プラスワンとして「誰と？」や「いつ？」といった質問をしてみましょう。

17 A new holiday or festival

一問一答　3分×8回　まとめ　目安20分

新しい祝日

実施おすすめ学年

1年	2年	3年
◎	○	○

使用する文法事項

be 動詞，一般動詞現在形
など

毎回1つずつ，3分間で質問に答えましょう！

1. Please make a new holiday or festival. What is the name of the new holiday or festival?
2. What is it about?
3. When is the holiday?
4. How do you celebrate it?
5. What else do you do?
6. Where is it held?
7. What is its decoration?
8. What is its traditional food?

※未習の文法を含む質問はカットするか，既習文法を用いた同意の質問に作りかえるなどアレンジしてください。

Ⓐ 一問一答の解答例

1. It is called, "Technology Day."
2. It is about the good things of technology.
3. It is on September 13th.
4. You must use a phone or computer to see the events.
5. You can play games with friends or visit museums.
6. It is everywhere in Japan.
7. Pictures of computers and posters of technology.
8. Gray food.

Ⓐ まとめ英作文の例

　The new holiday is called "Technology Day" and <u>it is about the good things of technology</u>. It is celebrated because technology has been a very useful thing for humans.

　It is celebrated on September 13th every year. There is no work and no school. On that day, <u>you must use a computer or a smartphone to see the events</u>. You see the events on the TV too!

　You can play computer games with friends. So, it is a holiday that is popular with children. You can also visit science museums. You will learn many things. It is held everywhere in Japan. There are a lot of pictures of computers and posters of technology on walls.

　Traditional food on that day is all kinds of gray food. Konyaku is very popular.

⚠ 指導上の留意点

　新しい休日を作ってみましょう、というテーマです。日本の祝祭日は2017年現在17日あります。これは世界的に見ても多いそうです。それだけでなく日本には「○○の日」のような「記念日」がたくさん存在しています。それに倣い、何かを祝う日、もしくは何かのお祭りの日として休日を新たに設定してみましょう。

　特別な日には、何か特別な飾りものをしたり、何か特別な料理を作って食べたりします。服装もいつもと違うものを着ることだってあります。そうした「しきたり」を自分で考え、英語で書いていくのです。

　文法的には、when, where, how, whatなど数種類の疑問詞が「一問一答」で用いられますが、それ以外には別段難しい文法は用いていませんので、疑問詞を一通り学習し終えた1年生に対して、最も適したテーマかもしれません。日付も1年生で学習しますのでちょうどよいと思います。

　Q7では受動態を用いた質問 Where is it held? がありますが、受動態が未習であれば、Where can you enjoy the holiday or festival? のように言い換えてしまってよいでしょう。

➕1 センテンス

　Q4やQ5は、お祝い事の内容を詳しく説明する場面です。机間巡視しながら Then? (それから？) と投げかけて、どんどん書かせていきましょう。

Chapter 2　表現力大幅アップ！3分英作文　おすすめテーマ　57

18 The food I hate the most

一問一答
3分×7回
まとめ
目安20分

この食べ物が大っ嫌い！

実施おすすめ学年

1年	2年	3年
○	◎	○

使用する文法事項

feel C，接続詞 if，like ～ better than ～ など

毎回1つずつ，3分間で質問に答えましょう！

1. What food do you hate the most?
2. Why do you hate it?
3. When/where did you eat it for the first time?
4. How did you feel then?
5. What do you usually do when it is served?
6. Which do you like better, eating the food or taking a test?
7. If you get money if you eat the food, how much do you want? And how will you eat it?

※未習の文法を含む質問はカットするか，既習文法を用いた同意の質問に作りかえるなどアレンジしてください。

Ⓐ 一問一答の解答例

1. Wasabi is the food I hate the most.
2. It is too spicy.
3. I don't remember my first time. I think it is at a sushi restaurant.
4. I felt surprised and angry.
5. I don't eat it at all.
6. Eating wasabi is easier than taking a test.
7. If I eat it, I want to get 5,000 yen. I will eat it fast!

Ⓐ まとめ英作文の例

　I like Japanese food. I eat it every day. But wasabi is the food I hate the most. It is too spicy for me! I don't remember my first time. I think it is at a sushi restaurant. It is usually eaten with sushi. Everyone eats it, so I tried it. I put wasabi on my sushi and I ate it. Then it happened. I was surprised and angry. My mouth was really painful! So, I don't eat it at all now. Sometimes, I eat sushi with wasabi in it.

　I get angry when I eat wasabi. But I think eating wasabi is easier than taking a test. Tests are difficult! Eating wasabi is faster than studying. Eating it is only a few seconds. But I have to study for a long time! If I eat it, I want to get 5,000 yen. I will eat it fast!

⚠ 指導上の留意点

　「好きな食べ物」というのは「3分英作文」でなくとも英作文指導のテーマとしてはポピュラーなものです。しかし今回の「嫌いな食べ物」というのはどうでしょう？　日本全国を探しても「嫌いな食べ物」を英作文のテーマに書かせたことのある先生方はあまりいないのではないでしょうか。

　しかし，好きなものの理由は「好きだから」としか言えないと思いますが，嫌いな理由ならたくさん書けるのです。筆者も，犬が好きな理由は好きだからとしか言えませんが，猫が嫌いな理由はいくらでも挙げられます。（猫好きな先生にはスミマセン）

　今まで指導した中で最も傑作だったのは，納豆が嫌いだという生徒がその理由として"because natto beans look like beatle's eggs!"と書いてきたことです。「納豆がカブトムシの卵だなんて！」と思いますが，納豆が嫌いなあの生徒にとってはそう見えるのだということです。こういう表現が自然に出てくるテーマ「嫌いな食べ物」。ぜひやってみてください。

➕1 センテンス

　Q4では，And what did you do after eating the food?　という質問を投げかけてあげれば，よりプラスワンセンテンスが出てくるかと思います。嫌いな食べ物をはじめて食べた時の衝撃を，英語で詳しく書かせてみましょう。

19 My future self

一問一答
3分×7回
まとめ
目安20分

私の未来予想図

実施おすすめ学年

1年	2年	3年
	◎	○

使用する文法事項

want to ~, have to ~, 接続詞 if,
一般動詞過去形
など

毎回1つずつ，3分間で質問に答えましょう！

1. What do you want to be in the future?
2. Tell us about it.
3. When did you decide it?
4. Why do you want to be one?
5. What do you have to do to be one?
6. Is it difficult for you to do it?
7. If you become one, what will you do then?

※未習の文法を含む質問はカットするか，既習文法を用いた同意の質問に作りかえるなどアレンジしてください。

A 一問一答の解答例

1. I want to be a YouTuber.
2. My videos will be very interesting. I want to make people happy.
3. When I saw a lot of great YouTube videos, I thought they were amazing. Now, I want to make videos too.
4. I can be rich!
5. I have to make a lot of interesting videos.
6. Yes, I have to start soon.
7. I can work at home and get money. It is a fun life!

A まとめ英作文の例

　I want to be a famous Youtuber. I will be famous because my videos will be very interesting. I will have a lot of fans. I will play games and talk about many things.

　I have a computer at home. It is a powerful computer. My father bought it. I will work hard and be more interesting. I want to make people happy. They are my fans. When I saw a lot of great Youtube videos, I thought they were amazing. I watch them every day.

　Now, I want to make videos too. If I make videos, I will get money. I can be rich! But I have to make a lot of interesting videos. So, I have to start soon. I think my first video is a singing video. It is very easy to do. Then, I can work at home and get money. I think it will be a fun life!

⚠ 指導上の留意点

　「将来の夢」を作文させることは，2年生の英語の授業では定番メニューだと思います。2年生では to 不定詞を学習しますので，want to を使った表現活動として「将来の夢」を作文として書かせ，スピーチまで持っていくというのが普通の流れだと思います。

　3分英作文でも将来の夢は「定番テーマ」として，to 不定詞を学習した後ならばいつでも，どんな生徒に対しても活用できるものだと思います。

　将来の夢，について具体的に理由や動機，実現に向けてのプランなどを日本語でも書いたことがない生徒は多いかと思います。また，クラスメイトが将来の夢をどのように抱いているのかを聴き合って自分の将来の参考にする，ということもあまりしないことだと思います。

　3分英作文では，英語を通して，自分の将来に対する希望や課題を整理し，具体的に述べさせることができるだけでなく，鑑賞会などの「交流」を通じてクラスメイトの将来に対する考えを知ることができます。

　そしてまた，クラスメイトの考えを知ることによって，自分の考えをもっと深めていくことができるのです。

➕1 センテンス

　Q3は将来の夢を決めるきっかけとなる出来事を聞く質問です。複数の文でより具体的に書いてみるよう呼びかけてみましょう。

20 The country I want to visit

一問一答
3分×10回
まとめ
目安20分

行ってみたいなあの国へ

実施おすすめ学年

1年	2年	3年
	◎	○

使用する文法事項

to 不定詞名詞用法 (want to ～), to 不定詞形容詞用法, How long ～

毎回1つずつ，3分間で質問に答えましょう！

1. What country do you want to visit?
2. Why do you want to go there?
3. How long does it take to go there by plane?
4. What language do they speak?
5. What is a good spot to visit there?
6. Tell us about it.
7. What is the famous thing/food there?
8. Tell us about it.
9. Who do you want to go there with?
10. When is the best time to visit?

※未習の文法を含む質問はカットするか，既習文法を用いた同意の質問に作りかえるなどアレンジしてください。

Ⓐ 一問一答の解答例

1. I want to visit Italy.
2. Because it is beautiful and I like art, history, and food.
3. It takes about 17 hours by plane.
4. They speak Italian and a little English.
5. Venezia is a good place to visit.
6. It is called the City of Canals. It is very old and it has many beautiful buildings.
7. Gondolas are famous there.
8. They are small boats that people use to go around the city.
9. I want to go there with my family.
10. I think summer is the best time to visit!

Ⓐ まとめ英作文の例

　I want to visit Italy, because it is a beautiful country and I like art, history, and Italian food.
　It is far away from Japan. It takes about 17 hours by plane to get there. They speak Italian and a little English there. So I will try and learn Italian.
　Venezia is a good place to visit. It is called the City of Canals. It is very old and it has many beautiful buildings. Also, gondolas are famous there. They are small boats that people use to go around the city. There are no cars there.
　Roma and Firenze are also famous places there. I want to go there with my family. We will visit the famous places and take lots of pictures. I think that summer is the best time to visit!

⚠ 指導上の留意点

　「行ってみたい国」も、「将来の夢」と同じく want to 導入後にぜひ作文させたいテーマの一つです。今でこそ海外旅行は一般的なものとなり、若者があまり海外に対して強い興味を持たなくなってきているという傾向もあるようですが、それでも英語を学習する中学生に対し、世界に目を向けさせることは英語教師としての役目の一つであると思っています。

　このテーマでは「その国の公用語」「その国の観光スポット」「その国の有名なものや食べ物」を書く「一問一答」があります。いきなりこの質問を投げかけてもすぐに答えが出にくいことが予想されるのであれば、調べ学習としてパソコン室であらかじめ行きたい国について調べさせてもよいです。

　普段通りの「まとめ」のやり方でやっても構いませんが、「まとめ」の時間になったら大きな紙を渡し、新聞やポスターを作成させ、完成品を教室に掲示し、鑑賞会を開いて、最後にナンバーワンを決めるべく投票をさせる、といった活動に膨らませることもできます。

➕1 センテンス

　Q6, Q8に関しては、なかなか書けないようであれば What is the good point of it? のような質問をしてあげましょう。

21 The season I like the best

いちばん好きな季節

実施おすすめ学年

1年	2年	3年
	◎	○

使用する文法事項
最上級（like 〜 the best），feel C,
like to 〜，want to 〜
など

毎回1つずつ，3分間で質問に答えましょう！

1. What season do you like the best?
2. Why do you like it?
3. How do you feel during the season?
4. What do you like to/want to/usually eat then?
5. Where do you like to/want to/usually go then?
6. What do you like to/want to/usually do then?
7. What is the special event in that season?
8. Tell us about it.

※未習の文法を含む質問はカットするか，既習文法を用いた同意の質問に作りかえるなどアレンジしてください。

A 一問一答の解答例

1. I like fall the best of all seasons.
2. It is cool and it is not rainy. The colors of trees are pretty!
3. I feel so refreshed and happy.
4. I usually eat vegetables and hot stew.
5. I go to the mountains and parks with my friends or family to see the trees.
6. I like to watch the leaves and spend a slow relaxing time.
7. I go camping.
8. We go to a forest and stay outdoors. We have bonfire. It is fun!

A まとめ英作文の例

　I like fall the best of all seasons, because it is cool and it is not rainy. I don't like the hot weather. I don't like the wet weather too.

　When it is fall, the leaves change colors. The leaves are orange, red, and yellow. The colors of the trees are very pretty! I feel so refreshed and happy when I see them. Also, the food is delicious during this season. There are a lot of delicious fall dishes in Japan. I usually eat vegetables and hot stew. I like mushrooms too!

　I go to the mountains and parks with my friends or family to see the trees. Many people do it too. And I like to watch the leaves and spend a slow relaxing time. We usually go camping where we go to a forest and stay outdoors. We have bonfire and we cook food with it. It is fun! I love fall!

指導上の留意点

　日本は四季がはっきりしており，一つ一つの季節を感じやすい国です。さらにその季節ごとに行事や催事が多いです。そんな日本の特徴を生かした作文テーマだと思います。

　文法事項としては最上級を扱うので実施時期を２年生からとしましたが，Q１"What season do you like the best?"を，"What is your favorite season?"としてしまえば１年生からでもこのテーマを指導可能となります。本書で何度も触れていることですが，そうやって生徒の実態に応じていくらでもアレンジ可能なところが「３分英作文」の最大の特徴です。

　Q５・６に関しては「行くのが好きなところ（するのが好きなこと）」「行ってみたいところ（してみたいこと）」「普段行くところ（普段すること）」の３つの表現に幅を持たせています。例えば「行ってみたいところ（してみたいこと）」だけにしてしまうと「そんなものはない」という回答をしてしまう生徒も出てきてしまいます。だから３つ用意してみました。どれを書いてもよいですし，もちろん３つ全部書いてもよいと伝えましょう。

プラス１センテンス

　Q４，５，６については，答えに続けて理由も書くように伝えれば，プラスワンが出てくるかと思います。

22 The best school lunch

一問一答
3分×7回
まとめ
目安20分

マイベスト給食

実施おすすめ学年

1年	2年	3年
○	◎	○

使用する文法事項

want to, have to, 接続詞 if, 受動態, 最上級（like 〜 the best）
など

毎回1つずつ，3分間で質問に答えましょう！

1. Which do you like the best, bread, rice, or noodle? And what kind?
2. What is the main dish?
3. What is the side dish?
4. What is the dessert?
5. Which drink do you like, milk, coffee milk, or green tea?
6. If you can only eat it once a year, when do you want to eat it?
7. If this is served at a restaurant, how much is it?

※未習の文法を含む質問はカットするか，既習文法を用いた同意の質問に作りかえるなどアレンジしてください。

A 一問一答の解答例

1. I like bread the best. I like French bread the best.
2. The main dish is spaghetti with meat sauce and mushrooms.
3. The side dish is wakame salad with corn.
4. The dessert is yogurt. It is healthy.
5. I like coffee milk. It is sweet and delicious.
6. I want to eat it on my birthday.
7. The price is 500 yen.

A まとめ英作文の例

I like rice, bread, and noodles. But I like bread the best of all. I especially like French bread because it is soft and delicious.

The main dish that I want is spaghetti with meat sauce and mushrooms. I want a lot of sauce on it. I will eat the French bread with the spaghetti.

Then the side dish is wakame salad with corn. The dessert is yogurt because it is healthy too. I can eat a lot.

Lastly, the drink is coffee milk. I like it because it is sweet and delicious. But I don't drink coffee. Coffee is not delicious for me.

I want to eat this meal on my birthday. It will make me happy. If I am happy, my school life will be happy too. At a restaurant, I think the price of this is 500 yen. I think many people will buy it!

指導上の留意点

給食がない学校にお勤めの先生方には申し訳ないですが，給食がある学校の中学生にとっては，給食は学校生活の関心事の一つなのです。4時間目の授業にもなれば，教室に掲示された献立表をチラチラと見つめる生徒たち…。

そんな生徒たちの関心事である給食を「3分英作文」にしてみようというのがこのテーマです。好きな給食のメニューを並べた「マイベスト給食」を考えさせてみましょう。

なおQ2でmain dishというと「主食」と考えてriceやbreadと答えてしまう生徒がいますが，main dishは「主菜」です。ハンバーグや唐揚げ，サバの味噌煮といったものが給食のmain dishになってくるかと思います。

給食がない学校にお勤めの先生は"My best bento"でやってみるというのはどうでしょう。余談ですが，昼食はレストランで食べるか買って食べるという文化の欧米でも，近年弁当の文化が日本から輸入されているらしく，bentoという単語は認知度が上がってきているようです（eにアクセントがある）。

センテンス

Q5では，なぜその飲み物がいいのか理由も書かせてみましょう。単純に好きだからということもあるかもしれませんし，おかずとのバランスを考えて選んでいるかもしれません。

23 Who is your hero?

一問一答
3分×9回
まとめ
目安20分

私のヒーロー

実施おすすめ学年

1年	2年	3年
	◎	○

使用する文法事項

三人称単数現在，未来表現，want to ～，have to ～，接続詞 if，など

毎回1つずつ，3分間で質問に答えましょう！

1. Who is your hero? (Who do you admire?)
2. Where does he/she live?
3. How old is he/she?
4. What is his/her job?
5. When did he/she become your hero?
6. Why is he/she your hero?
7. What will you do if you meet him/her?
8. Do you want to be like him/her?
9. What do you have to do to be like him/her?

※未習の文法を含む質問はカットするか，既習文法を用いた同意の質問に作りかえるなどアレンジしてください。

A 一問一答の解答例

1. My hero is my brother.
2. He lives in Tokyo now.
3. He is 20 years old.
4. He is a student at a university.
5. He is my hero since I was a child.
6. Because he always takes care of me and he is the best!
7. I want to say thank you.
8. Yes, I do.
9. I must be kind to my family and helpful to others.

A まとめ英作文の例

My older brother is my hero. His name is Tadakatsu. He lives in an apartment in Tokyo now. He is twenty years old and a student at a university there. He wants to be a doctor, so he has to study very hard. He comes home during the holidays. He visits us often and gives omiyage to us. He always comes for birthdays. My older brother is my hero since I was a child. Because he always takes care of me. He is the best! We play many games, watch a lot of movies, and play different sports together.

He is always kind to me and our parents. I want to say thank you to him. I'm happy he is my brother. Also, I want to be like him. I want to be a good person too. So, I must be kind to my family and be helpful to others.

⚠ 指導上の留意点

自分が尊敬する人物 "My hero" について作文するテーマです。尊敬する人物であれば，誰でも構わないということにします。家族や身の回りの人物，芸能人，スポーツ選手，歴史上の人物，アニメや漫画の登場人物…生徒には意外にも，尊敬する人物がいるものです。

文法的には，このテーマが他人を紹介するテーマであるので，3人称を使います。まずはその尊敬する人物がどういう人物であるかを書かせ，最後には，なぜその人を尊敬しているのかだったり，その人に会ったら何をしたいかだったりと自分とその人物との関連性について書かせていきます。

「では，尊敬する人物について英語で書いてみましょう」と指示して白紙の原稿用紙を渡しても，生徒はなかなか書けないと思いますが，この「3分英作文」の「一問一答」から「まとめ」につなげていくという手法を取れば，比較的容易に書いていけるテーマになると思います。

➕1 センテンス

Q5は，より具体的に書かせるためにWhen? だけではなく，Where? や How? といった質問を投げかけてみましょう。

Q9に続いて，Q10として So, what will you do every day to be like him/her? のような質問をしてみてもよいでしょう。

24 I never leave home without…

一問一答
3分×7回
まとめ
目安20分

外出時に必ず持っていくもの

実施おすすめ学年

1年	2年	3年
	◎	○

使用する文法事項

I think ～，接続詞 if，接続詞 when など

毎回1つずつ，3分間で質問に答えましょう！

1. What do you always carry when you go out?
2. When/where did you get it?
3. Why do you always carry it with you?
4. How do you use it?
5. What will you do if you left it at home?
6. Do you think other people should use it too?
7. If you can make one, what will you change in it?

※未習の文法を含む質問はカットするか，既習文法を用いた同意の質問に作りかえるなどアレンジしてください。

A 一問一答の解答例

1. I always carry my smartphone.
2. I got it from my parents.
3. It is very useful.
4. I talk with my friends and I play games.
5. I will go home and get it.
6. Yes, I do. It is a great invention.
7. I will make it very strong and it will never break.

A まとめ英作文の例

　<u>I always carry my smartphone</u>. <u>I got it from my parents</u>. They are the best parents in the world. They gave it to me for my birthday. It is very convenient and useful. I can do many things with it. <u>I talk with my friends and I play</u> a lot of good <u>games</u>. Sometimes, we play together too. I can study and learn through the Internet. There are many sites that help me with my homework. I use it to understand difficult problems. I really use it a lot!

　If I don't have it, I have to go home and get it. I don't want to go out without my phone. <u>It is a great invention</u>. But if I can make one, <u>I will make it very strong and it will never break</u>! I will sell it at a low price, so many people can buy it and use it.

⚠ 指導上の留意点

　外出時に必ず持っていくものを英作文します。人によって様々なものを携行していくと思いますが，中学生ならではの携行品があると思います。たいていのオトナはスマホを携行していくのでしょうが，スマホやケータイを持っていない中学生もいるはずで，そんな人は何を肌身離さずに持ち歩くのでしょうか。そんな中学生の日常生活を覗き見することができそうなテーマとなっています。

　筆者がこのテーマを試してみた時は，実に様々な携行品が出てきました。財布，筆箱，ノート，小説…勉強熱心なある生徒は「参考書」と書いていてクラスメイトをびっくりさせていました（笑）。

　使用する文法事項には，特に難しいものがありませんので，「一問一答」を工夫すれば１年生でも十分に対応できるテーマです。下記の一問一答例ではI think や if を使用していますが，１年生でも解答可能な質問に変えればよいのです。

　「交流」の仕方としては，絵を描かせてスピーチにしてもよいですし，鑑賞会としてクラスメイトの作品を読み合って感想を描かせるという方法でもよいでしょう。

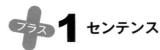
プラス1 センテンス

　Q3，Q4あたりでは，生徒の思いが強く表れてくる質問だと思います。最低２文は書いてみるように伝えましょう。

25 I don't want to do it!

一問一答 3分×6回 まとめ 目安20分

こんなことはやりたくない！

実施おすすめ学年

1年	2年	3年
	◎	○

使用する文法事項

want to ～, have to ～, feel C, 接続詞 if
など

毎回1つずつ，3分間で質問に答えましょう！

1. What don't you want to do the most?
2. Why don't you want to do it?
3. How will you feel if you do it?
4. What will happen if you don't do it?
5. What will happen if you do it?
6. Do you have to do it? Why or why not?

※未習の文法を含む質問はカットするか，既習文法を用いた同意の質問に作りかえるなどアレンジしてください。

Ⓐ 一問一答の解答例

1. I don't want to study too much.
2. It will make me tired and unhealthy.
3. I will feel very very sad.
4. I will not get money.
5. I will get money and get tired and sad.
6. Yes, I do. Because I need money.

Ⓐ まとめ英作文の例

　<u>I don't want to study too much</u>, because I think studying for a long time is not good. We must finish my homework in a short time. But in Japan, students have to do much homework. They study for many hours. My older brother who is a high school student studies a lot too, so he is always busy.

　I think studying <u>will make us tired and unhealthy</u>. If I study for a long time, <u>I will feel very sad</u>. But if I don't study, I will not enter a high school. It is a big problem! I need to go to a high school.

　Anyway, I have to study because I really need to go to a high school. So, I will study hard but I will finish my homework fast. Then, I will play games. I think I can be happy.

⚠ 指導上の留意点

　want to を導入した後に,「やりたいこと」はよく英作文のテーマにすると思います。今回はその逆で,「やりたくないこと」を英作文させてみましょう。

　これは「嫌いな食べ物」のテーマでも触れましたが, 人の習性として「好きなものより嫌いなものの方が, 人に伝えたい欲求が強い」「好きなものより嫌いなものの方が, より鮮明に覚えていて, そのため描写が詳しくなる」というのがあるからです。

　文法的には want to や if が登場しますので, ２年生向けのテーマと言えます。２学期には to 不定詞を学習すると思いますので, その復習として行ってもいいですし, より表現が豊かになってきた３年生になってから行ってもいいと思います。

　中学生もいろいろ苦手なもの, やりたくないものがあるそうです。「長距離走をしたくない」「テスト勉強したくない」「家事をしたくない」などに始まり, 極めて個人的な話題でやりたくないものを挙げてくる生徒もいます。

➕1 センテンス

　Q3は, 特にいつやりたくないと思うか？のような付加的な質問をすることでプラスワンを引き出すことができます。

　Q7では, しなければならないと思うかどうかと, その理由も聞いているので, その２つの質問に答えるだけでプラスワンができると思います。

26 Format for debate

ディベートのお作法

実施おすすめ学年

1年	2年	3年
	◎	○

使用する文法事項

want to 〜，have to 〜，接続詞 if，比較級（like 〜 better than 〜），think 〜 など

毎回1つずつ，3分間で質問に答えましょう！

1. Which do you like better, <u>anime</u> or <u>manga</u>?
   ※下線部をいろいろ変えてみましょう。
2. Do you think other people like it too?
3. What are the good points of it?
4. How about the other one?
5. But what are the bad points of it?
6. How about the other one?
7. What is a good example of it?
8. Why is that a good example?

※未習の文法を含む質問はカットするか，既習文法を用いた同意の質問に作りかえるなどアレンジしてください。

Ⓐ 一問一答の解答例

1. I like anime better than manga.
2. Yes, I do. Many people like anime.
3. Anime is fun and it is easy to enjoy.
4. Manga is also fun and it is usually the complete story.
5. Anime sometimes changes the original story.
6. You need a lot of time to read a manga.
7. Dragon ball.
8. It is a very famous anime and manga all over the world.

Ⓐ まとめ英作文の例

　I like anime better than manga. I always watch anime at home. Sometimes, I watch anime on my phone. I think many people also like anime better, because anime is fun and it is easy to enjoy. There are many shows you can watch. I like to watch fantasy and adventure shows.

　Manga is also fun and it is usually the complete story. It is expensive to buy them, so I like anime better. But anime sometimes change the original story and you need a lot of time and money to read manga.

　Anyway, Dragon ball is a good example. Do you know it? Dragon ball's anime is more famous than its manga all over the world. Many people watch Dragon ball. I'm a big fan too. Some anime shows are in English and other languages. So it is easy to watch and enjoy.

⚠ 指導上の留意点

　英語の授業でディベートをする機会はこれから増えてくると思います。というのは，平成29年版の学習指導要領では「話すこと」の領域がさらに細かく「発表」と「やり取り」に分かれるからです。

　つまり，スピーチ活動などをさせる「発表」と，チャットやディベートなどの「やり取り」の両方の技能を育成していかなければなりません。

　筆者も正直なところ，チャットはともかく，中学生にディベートをさせるのはとても負荷が高く，実施するのが難しいと思っています。そのハードルの高さを少しでも低くしようと思い，「3分英作文」でディベートの「台本」を作成させてから実施してみようというアイデアが浮かびました。

　もちろんここで紹介するのは，本格的なものではなく，あくまでも簡易的なものですが，これをきっかけとして，少しずつ難易度の高いディベートを行ってみてください。

　また，このフォーマットを使って英作文をさせるだけで，論理的な文章構成も身についてくると思います。比較級を学習した後の2年生にぜひ，チャレンジさせてみてください。

➕1 センテンス

　Q5，Q6は自分が選んだ側の欠点を挙げさせます。それに対する解決策もプラスワンで書かせてみるといいかもしれません。

27 The bad time

一問一答
3分×6回
まとめ
目安20分

最悪の瞬間

実施おすすめ学年

1年	2年	3年
	◎	○

使用する文法事項

want to ～, have to ～, 接続詞 if, 一般動詞過去形
など

毎回1つずつ，3分間で質問に答えましょう！

1. When was your worst day ever?
2. How did you feel then?
3. Where did it happen?
4. What happened on that day?
5. Why do you think it happened?
6. If you can do the day again, what will you do?

※未習の文法を含む質問はカットするか，既習文法を用いた同意の質問に作りかえるなどアレンジしてください。

Ⓐ 一問一答の解答例

1. My worst day was the day that we moved to a new house.
2. I was sad and worried. I didn't like it.
3. We moved to Iruma. Everything was new and scary.
4. I said goodbye to my friends. I cried a lot.
5. We changed houses because my father has a new job. So, I changed schools too.
6. I would not worry because I love Iruma now.

Ⓐ まとめ英作文の例

My worst day was the day that we moved to a new house. I liked our old house. It was big and has a beautiful garden. My room was big too. So, I was very sad and worried. I didn't want to move to a new house. I didn't like it. But we moved to Iruma.

Everything was new and scary then. I didn't know anyone in Iruma. I said goodbye to my friends and I cried a lot. They cried a lot too.

We changed houses because my father has a new job. So, I changed schools too. It was very difficult for me. It was hard to make new friends.

Anyway, I would not worry because I love Iruma now. This is a nice city and my classmates are my friends. I want to take my old friends here!

⚠ 指導上の留意点

「人生最悪の瞬間」を書いてもらうのが、このテーマです。

人間の習性として、幸せな瞬間よりも、不幸せな瞬間の方がよく覚えており、しかも、その不幸を自慢（？）したくなるというのがあると思いませんか。その「発信したい願望」「人に伝えたい気持ち」を、英作文で叶えてあげましょう。

例えば「３分英作文」のテーマの一つに「嫌いな食べ物」を書かせるというのがありますが、それと同じで、好きなものより嫌いなもの、幸せなことより不幸せなこと、の方が、作文させるととても詳しく書けてしまうものなのです。

テーマとしても「好きな〇〇」といった作文テーマばかりでは、生徒は飽きてしまうものです。たまにはこういう奇をてらったテーマはいかがでしょうか。

また、このテーマをやって一番盛り上がるのが「鑑賞会」です。人の失敗、人の不幸というものはなんで面白いのでしょうね。クラスメイトの「最悪の瞬間」を読んだり聞いたりして、教室は爆笑すること間違いなしですよ。

➕1 センテンス

Q4で詳しく書かせるためには、机間巡視しながら適宜 "When?" "Why?" "Where?" "Write the story more." などを生徒につぶやいてみましょう。

28 If you can go back in time…

一問一答
3分×9回
まとめ
目安20分

もしもあの時に戻れたら…？

実施おすすめ学年

1年	2年	3年
	◎	○

使用する文法事項

want to ～，have to ～，接続詞 if，過去進行形，未来表現
など

毎回1つずつ，3分間で質問に答えましょう！

1. What moment do you want to visit again?
2. How old were you then?
3. What were you doing?
4. Why did you choose that time?
5. What will you do while you are there again?
6. Will you change the events? How?
7. Do you want to stay there? Why?
8. What will happen to your present self?
9. Give a message to your past self.

※未習の文法を含む質問はカットするか，既習文法を用いた同意の質問に作りかえるなどアレンジしてください。

Ⓐ 一問一答の解答例

1. I want to visit the time that I was in Europe.
2. I was 10 years old then.
3. I went to many countries with my family.
4. It was a very fun and exciting trip. I had a wonderful experience.
5. I will enjoy more things and take a lot of pictures.
6. No, I will not. Our trip was perfect.
7. Yes, I do. I want to do it again.
8. I will have great memories.
9. "Enjoy the trip!"

Ⓐ まとめ英作文の例

　I want to visit the time that I was in Europe. I was 10 years old then. I went to many countries with my family. We went to the UK, France and Italy. We went there by plane and then by train. It was a very fun and exciting trip. I was tired, but I had a wonderful experience. We went to famous places and ate delicious dishes. I saw amazing things every day.
　If I did it again, I would enjoy more things and take a lot of pictures. I will not change anything, because our trip was perfect. So, I want to do it again.
　I want to take my friends and family there. They will like it very much. We will have great memories. If I can give a message to my past self, I want to say "Enjoy the trip!"

⚠ 指導上の留意点

　もし，過去のあの頃に戻ることができたなら…というテーマです。

　もしあの時に戻ることができたなら，あんな失敗はしないだろう，もしあの時に戻ることができたなら，あの楽しかった出来事をもう1回味わうことができる，などなど，中学生は13～15年しか生きていませんが，きっと「あの時ああしていれば」とか「あの時をもう1回味わいたい」といった思いがあるはずです。その思いを英作文で存分に書いてもらいましょう。

　内容としては，まず，過去のどの時点に戻りたいかを尋ねます（Q1），さらに，もし戻ったら何をしたいかを尋ねていきます（Q5）最後に，その頃の自分にメッセージを送って（Q9），このテーマの終わりとします。

　文法的には未来のwillを用いますので，2年生が適しているかと思いますが，3年生にも十分楽しんでもらえるテーマだと思います。

プラス1センテンス

　Q6では，もし過去を変えたいと思っているのであれば，How? と，どのように過去を変えていくのかを書かせます。逆に，過去を変えたいと思わないのであれば，Why? と聞いてみましょう。プラスワンがそこで出てくるかと思います。

29 My school trip

一問一答
3分×12回
まとめ
目安20分

校外学習（修学旅行）の思い出

実施おすすめ学年

1年	2年	3年
	◎	○

使用する文法事項

want to ～, have to ～, 接続詞 if
一般動詞過去形
など

毎回1つずつ，3分間で質問に答えましょう！

1. Where did you go?
2. Who went there with you?
3. When did you go there?
4. How long did you stay there?
5. How did you go there? By train or bus?
6. Where did you go on the first day?
7. What did you do there?
8. Where did you go on the second day?
9. What did you do there?
10. What was the best food there?
11. What did you learn through this trip?
12. Do you want to go there again?

※未習の文法を含む質問はカットするか，既習文法を用いた同意の質問に作りかえるなどアレンジしてください。

A 一問一答の解答例

1. I went to Kyoto and Nara.
2. I went with my classmates and teachers.
3. I went there last month.
4. For three days.
5. By train and bus.
6. I went to Nara.
7. I gave food to some deer.
8. I went to many temples in Kyoto.
9. I took some pictures.
10. I ate nama yatsuhashi.
11. I learned about Japanese history.
12. Yes, I do.

A まとめ英作文の例

I'm going to talk about my school trip. I went to Kyoto and Nara with my classmates and teachers last month. I was really excited about it.

We stayed there for three days. We went there by train and bus. The Shinkansen is really fast! It was my first time to ride it. On the first day, we went to Nara and gave food to some deer. I gave them shika-senbei. They were very cute.

On the second day, we went to many temples in Kyoto. I saw Kiyomizu and Kinkaku-ji and took some pictures. They were so beautiful. I ate nama yatsuhash. I bought some for my family too. I learned about Japanese history on our trip. After that, we went back home. So, I want to go there again someday.

⚠ 指導上の留意点

遠足や宿泊学習，修学旅行などの旅行的行事の後に，その思い出を英語で作文させるためのテーマです。

特に学校での校外学習に限った質問をしているわけではありませんので，夏休みや冬休みなどの長期休暇の後，新学期最初の授業から「長期休暇の思い出」をテーマにこの一問一答をしてもよいと思います。

このテーマは思い出を書くわけですから，過去形での「一問一答」がほとんどになります。したがって，過去形を学習した後に行うべきテーマとなります。

Where, Who, When, How, How long, What といった疑問文が出てきますので，復習をするにはとてもよいテーマにもなっています。

ここでは一泊二日であることを想定してQ7～9を作成しましたが，二泊三日であればQ10，11を付け足せばよいですし，日帰りであればQ8，9を削除してください。

➕1 センテンス

Q7，Q9では，実際に何をしたのかを書かせます。時系列順に何をしたのかを書かせるだけでなく，How did you feel then? のような質問をして，事実の羅列だけにならないようにしましょう。

30 Welcome to Japan!

一問一答
3分×10回
まとめ
目安20分

外国人の友達をお・も・て・な・し！

実施おすすめ学年

1年	2年	3年
	◎	○

使用する文法事項
未来表現，接続詞 if，How long ～ など

毎回1つずつ，3分間で質問に答えましょう！

1. If you have a foreigner friend, where is he/she from?
2. How did you meet each other?
3. If he/she visits Japan, where will you take him/her?
4. How will you go there?
5. How long will you stay there?
6. What will you do there?
7. What dishes will you eat there?
8. What is a good souvenir from that place?
9. What is another place he/she should visit next?
10. Before they leave Japan, teach them a Japanese word.

※未習の文法を含む質問はカットするか，既習文法を用いた同意の質問に作りかえるなどアレンジしてください。

A 一問一答の解答例

1. She is from America.
2. We met online and sent e-mails to each other.
3. I will take her to Kyoto.
4. We will go by shinkansen.
5. About one week.
6. We will visit many famous places there.
7. We will eat a lot of Japanese dishes and sweets.
8. I think it is yatsuhashi.
9. Tokyo city is a good place to visit too.
10. "Yoroshiku!"

A まとめ英作文の例

My friend is from America. She is an American and she is very cute and kind. We met online and sent e-mails to each other. We talk every day. So, we became friends very fast.

I want her to visit Japan. If she visits Japan, I will take her to Kyoto. I think it is one of the most beautiful cities in the world. It is my favorite place in Japan.

We will go by shinkansen. It takes about an hour and a half to go there from Tokyo. We will stay for about one week and visit many famous places there. I will take her to Kiyomizu Temple. We will eat a lot of Japanese dishes and sweets. I think yatsuhashi is a famous Kyoto souvenir.

Tokyo city is a good place to visit too. There are many exciting things to do in Tokyo. Lastly, I will teach her "Yoroshiku!"

⚠ 指導上の留意点

「もしも外国人の友達が日本に来たら，どんなおもてなしをしますか？」というテーマです。現実にありそうでなかなかないシチュエーションを想像して，実際に書いてみるということです。

こういうシチュエーションは，だいたいどの教科書でも似たようなストーリーがあります。ですから，そういうストーリーを学習した後に，「君たちだったらどうする？」というような流れでこのテーマに取り組んでも面白いと思います。

また，こういうテーマに取り組ませることで，改めて日本の文化や歴史に着目させるという意味もあります。単純に「日本のいいところを紹介しよう！」という英作文テーマで取り組ませるよりも「外国人の友達をおもてなししよう！」の方が，より具体的なタスクとなり，生徒の関心意欲を引くことになります。

なお，筆者は「日本国内であればどこへ案内してもよい」ということにしていますが，より郷土に関心を向けさせたいのであれば，「○○市・××県を案内しよう」という「縛り」を設けてもよいと思います。

センテンス

Q6では，外国から来た友達と何をするかを尋ねています。ここは具体的に書けるところですので，ぜひ2文以上書かせることにチャレンジさせてみてください。

31 A useful machine

一問一答
3分×10回
まとめ
目安20分

新しい家電製品を発明しよう！

実施おすすめ学年

1年	2年	3年
	◎	○

使用する文法事項

過去形，助動詞 should，How often 〜，助動詞 can，How much 〜，三人称単数現在
など

毎回1つずつ，3分間で質問に答えましょう！

1. What is the name of this machine?
2. Where/when did you buy it?
3. How much is it?
4. What can it do?
5. How do you use it?
6. Why did you get it?
7. When do you use it?
8. How often do you use it?
9. Does your family use it?
10. Should other people use it too?

※未習の文法を含む質問はカットするか，既習文法を用いた同意の質問に作りかえるなどアレンジしてください。

A 一問一答の解答例

1. This is a Cold Oven.
2. I bought it at a special store.
3. It is about 10,000 yen.
4. It can make dishes cold very quickly.
5. You put the food inside and choose the time.
6. Because I like cold desserts.
7. I usually use it during summer.
8. I use it almost every day.
9. Yes, they do.
10. Yes, they should try it.

A まとめ英作文の例

This is a Cold Oven. It looks like a normal oven. But it is the most amazing machine! I bought it at a special store. The store has a lot of other amazing machines. But I like this one the best of all. It is about 10,000 yen. It is expensive but it is really useful.

It can make dishes cold very quickly. Just put the food inside and choose the time. After a few minutes, the food will become cold. If you choose a longer time, it will become colder. Magic, right?

For example, if you put hot coffee, it will become cold coffee. Then, if you put cold coffee again, it will become iced coffee! I like cold food and drinks, so I usually use it during summer.

Actually, I use it almost every day and during winter! My family uses it too. I think you should try it too!

指導上の留意点

もし，こんな新しい機械があったら…。という想像力を働かせて作文をするテーマです。世の中はとても便利になりました。様々な機械が世に出され，自動車でさえ近い将来は自分で運転する必要が完全になくなるかもしれません。我々が快適に生活をすることができるのは，実に様々な機械が発明され，それを利用しているからです。

そこで，中学生の自由な発想で，新しい家電製品を開発してもらいましょう。「こんな家電製品があったらいいな」というテーマで，実際にその家電製品を持っていて，実際に使っているというシチュエーションで「3分英作文」をしてもらいます。

「作品例」では「冷たい食べ物を作るオーブン」について書かれていますが，他にも筆者が指導した生徒は「自動で体を洗ってくれるロボット」「材料を入れるだけで料理を作ってくれる機械」「宿題をやってくれるロボット」などを書いていました

このテーマでは絵を描かせると，生徒の創作をより活発なもの・具体的なものにできるかと思います。最初に描かせても最後に描かせても構いません。

Q4では，この機械で何ができるかを書きます。できるだけ2文以上で具体的に書いてみるように伝えてみましょう。

32 To be an animal

一問一答
3分×10回
まとめ
目安20分

動物に変身！

実施おすすめ学年

1年	2年	3年
	◎	○

使用する文法事項

未来表現，接続詞 if
など

毎回1つずつ，3分間で質問に答えましょう！

1. What is your favorite animal?
2. Why do you like it?
3. If you become that animal, what will you do?
4. Where will you live?
5. How will you live there?
6. What will you eat?
7. How will you get food and other things?
8. If another animal fights you, what will you do?
9. What will be your future?
10. What is the next best animal for you?

※未習の文法を含む質問はカットするか，既習文法を用いた同意の質問に作りかえるなどアレンジしてください。

Ⓐ 一問一答の解答例

1. My favorite animal is a cat.
2. Because they are pretty and soft.
3. I will sleep all day!
4. I will live in a big house.
5. I will live lazily.
6. I will eat cat food.
7. From a person or find it myself.
8. I will fight hard.
9. I will have a slow and peaceful life.
10. I like dogs too.

Ⓐ まとめ英作文の例

　<u>My favorite animal is a cat, because they are pretty and soft.</u> I have two cute cats at home. Their names are Bubu chan and Popo chan. If I became one, <u>I will sleep all day!</u> I like sleeping for many hours.

　<u>I will live in a big house and live lazily.</u> I will get cat food <u>from a person or find it myself.</u> I want to get expensive cat food. They look so delicious.

　I can fight hard and I will use my sharp teeth! I will scream very loud too. But I think <u>I will have a slow and peaceful life,</u> because my cats are very lazy now. I will be like my cats.

　Oh, I can be a dog too! I love playing outside all day. I am a very happy person. I like the life of a pet. It is fun and easy, but very short!

⚠ 指導上の留意点

「もし動物になれるとしたら，何になる？ そして，何をする？」というテーマです。まずは好きな動物を挙げてもらい，次にその動物になったら，どんなことをするか？

「シベリアンハスキーになって犬ソリのレースに出たい」「鳥になって空を飛んでみたい」「かわいい猫になってお金持ちの家に飼ってもらう」「ナマケモノになって，1日中寝ていたい」といったものが出てくるかもしれませんね。

文法的には，いわゆる「その場で決めた未来」である will を使っていきますので，2年生に向いているテーマと言えます。未来表現として2年生で be going to と will を学習しますが，その2つは厳密には同じ意味ではありません。be going to が「前から決めていた未来」であるのに対して，will は「その場で決めた未来」です。

ここでは「一問一答」で「もしこの動物になったら，何をする？」とその場で聞いているので，その場で「じゃあ，○○をする」と答えます。「何を食べる？」とその場で聞いているので「じゃあ，○○を食べる」と答えます。このやり取りにおいて使用する未来表現は will が適切であり，be going to に置き換えることはできません。

➕1 センテンス

Q3がこのテーマで最も重要な質問です。その動物になって何をしたいかを，具体的に書かせてみましょう。

33 Another life

一問一答
3分×12回
まとめ
目安20分

もしもアニメやマンガの世界に入ったら…？

実施おすすめ学年

1年	2年	3年
	◎	○

使用する文法事項

want to ～，接続詞 if
比較級（like ～ better than ～）
など

毎回1つずつ，3分間で質問に答えましょう！

1. Which do you like better, anime or manga?
2. What anime/manga do you like?
3. Why do you like it?
4. Who is your favorite character?
5. If you go into the story, who will you be?
6. What is your character's story?
7. Do you have any special talents or powers?
8. What will you do there?
9. Tell us about that world.
10. Will you change the story of the anime/manga?
11. Who will be your friend there?
12. Do you want to return to the real world?

※未習の文法を含む質問はカットするか，既習文法を用いた同意の質問に作りかえるなどアレンジしてください。

A 一問一答の解答例

1. I like anime.
2. My favorite is Dragon Ball
3. Because it is cool and exciting.
4. I like Gokuu
5. I will be Gokuu.
6. I'm the greatest fighter of all!
7. I have the strongest power.
8. I will practice hard and become stronger.
9. Everyone fights each other, so the strongest wins.
10. No, I won't. It's a great story.
11. Kuririn will be my friend.
12. Yes, I do.

A まとめ英作文の例

I like anime. My favorite is Dragon Ball because it is cool and exciting. I watch that anime often. I have watched it since I was in elementary school.

I like Gokuu the best of all the characters of Dragon Ball. He is a very strong character. He is very interesting and funny too. I will be the greatest fighter of all because I have the strongest power. But I will practice hard and become stronger.

Everyone fights each other, so the strongest wins.

I think Kuririn will be my friend someday. He is not as strong as me, but he is powerful too. We will fight many strong characters together. But I want to go back to the real world. Dragon Ball's world is very dangerous.

⚠ 指導上の留意点

「もしもアニメやマンガの世界に入ったら」というテーマです。中学生はアニメや漫画が好きです。自分の好きなアニメやマンガの世界に入り込み，自分の好きなキャラクターになりきってその世界で生活をするという設定です。

中学生に対しては子供っぽいテーマに見えるかもしれませんが，英語で作文をさせるので，難易度的にはちょうどよいものとなっていると思います。たくさん英文を書かせるコツとして，簡単かつ，生徒が書きたいと思えるようなテーマを設定することがあります。その意味で，今回のテーマは中学生にとって描きやすいものになっていると思います。

もし好きなアニメや漫画がないという生徒がいた場合は，アニメやマンガに限らずドラマや小説の世界でも構わないとします。いずれにしても現実の世界とは違う作り話の世界に入り込ませる設定で書かせるテーマとなっています。

文法的には，未来表現の will を使用するので，2年生から取り組むことのできるテーマになっています。will 以外は特に難しい文法がありませんので，とても簡単に取り組むことができます。

 センテンス

Q4では，Why do you like that character? といった質問を投げかけることでプラスワンを引き出すことが可能です。

34 Wish comes true

一問一答
3分×10回
まとめ
目安20分

もしも魔法のランプがあったら…？

実施おすすめ学年

1年	2年	3年
	◎	○

使用する文法事項

want to ～，have to ～，接続詞 if,
feel c
など

毎回1つずつ，3分間で質問に答えましょう！

1. You have a magic lamp. You can have only three wishes. So, what is your first wish?
2. Why is it your wish?
3. What is your next wish?
4. Why is it your wish?
5. What is your last wish?
6. Why is it your wish?
7. What will happen if they all come true?
8. How will you feel after that?
9. If there is no magic, are your wishes possible?
10. If you can have only one wish, what is it?

※未習の文法を含む質問はカットするか，既習文法を用いた同意の質問に作りかえるなどアレンジしてください。

A 一問一答の解答例

1. I want to be smart.
2. Because I can get very rich.
3. I want to be handsome.
4. Because it is very cool and great.
5. I want to have a great body.
6. Because a rich and handsome man with a great body is the best.
7. My life is perfect forever.
8. I will be the happiest person in the world!
9. I can get money and a great body. But I can't become handsome.
10. I want to be happy.

A まとめ英作文の例

　If I have three wishes, first, <u>I want to be smart</u>. If I'm smart, <u>I can get very rich</u>. I will open my own company and make a lot of money. I will be a smart business man.

　Second, <u>I want to be handsome because it is very cool and great</u>. I think people will like me because I am handsome. I will be a famous star and be popular.

　Third, <u>I want to have a great body because</u> I think having big muscles is the best. I can play many kinds of sports. I will be smart, rich, handsome, and have a great body. Then, my life will be perfect forever. I will be the happiest person in the world!

⚠ 指導上の留意点

　ランプをこすると，煙とともにランプの精が飛び出して，3つの願い事を叶えてくれる。もし，そんな魔法のランプがあったなら，どんな願い事をしますか？ このテーマは，生徒の想像力・発想力をフル活用させるテーマです。

T : "You have a magic lamp. If you scrub the lamp, the god of lamp will come out of the lamp. And he will make your wishes come true. But you can have only three wishes. So, what will you wish?"
S : "I can't decide!"

　文法的には「願い事」なので，want toやwish toを使用する機会が増えるはずです。そこで，この文法事項の復習として，2年生に対してこのテーマをやってみるのが基本となるでしょう。もちろん，語彙など含めた総合的な表現力がついてきている3年生を相手にこのテーマを課しても面白いと思います。

➕1 センテンス

　Q7では願い事が全てかなったらどうなるかという質問をしています。なかなか思い浮かばないようなら，Then, what will you do? という質問をしてみましょう。

35 My superpower

一問一答
3分×10回
まとめ
目安20分

もしも私がスーパーヒーローだったら…？

実施おすすめ学年

1年	2年	3年
	◎	○

使用する文法事項

want to ～，will，接続詞 if，be going to ～，一般動詞過去形
など

毎回1つずつ，3分間で質問に答えましょう！

1. If you are a superhero, what is your name?
2. Tell us about your costume.
3. What is your superpower?
4. How did you get your power?
5. What will you do with it?
6. What is your weak point?
7. Who will you fight?
8. Do you have a partner or a group?
9. What will happen to the world?
10. Are you going to be good or evil?

※未習の文法を含む質問はカットするか，既習文法を用いた同意の質問に作りかえるなどアレンジしてください。

A 一問一答の解答例

1. I'm a Time God.
2. I wear a black and purple costume. I have gold eyes.
3. I can go slow and fast. I can go to the past or to the future.
4. My watch was hit by lightning.
5. I will travel to the past and future.
6. I must sleep 10 hours every day.
7. I will fight people who did bad things and people who will do bad things.
8. No, I am alone.
9. It will be very peaceful.
10. I think I will be a good superhero.

A まとめ英作文の例

　I'm a Time God. I wear a black and purple costume. It is a long coat and looks very cool. I have gold eyes and they shine. I can go slow or fast and I can go to the past or to the future.

　I got my power when my watch was hit by lightning. It was painful at first, but I'm okay. My watch is now powerful.

　I will use it to control time. Then, I will travel to the past and future. It is a great adventure. I will see many places at different times. But I must sleep 10 hours every day.

　I hide when I sleep. I will fight people who already did bad things and people who will do bad things alone. The world will be very peaceful because I think I will be a good superhero.

⚠ 指導上の留意点

　もしも，ある日突然自分に特別な力が宿り，スーパーヒーローになることができたなら…。このテーマは，スーパーヒーローになりきって，自分にどんな力があり，それを使って誰と戦い，何をしていくのかということを英語で答えていきます。注意点としては，全く新しいヒーローを創り出すということです。実在するアニメやテレビ番組のヒーローに自分がなるわけではありません。自分でコスチュームや能力を考えて，新しいヒーローを誕生させるのです。そこに中学生の発想力・表現力を広げるチャンスがあるのです。

　筆者がこのテーマで指導した時は，「ただただご飯を食べ続けるだけのヒーロー」「１分だけ空を飛べるヒーロー」「自分は何もできないけれど，世界中の有名なヒーローをいつでも呼ぶことができるヒーロー」と言った，なんだかちょっぴり面白いヒーローが続々と誕生しました。

　文法的には，未来のwillを用いる程度で，別段難しい文法を用いなくても十分に英作文可能なテーマです。２年生であれば難なく取り組めるものですし，がんばれば１年生にでも書けるテーマだと思います。

➕１ センテンス

　Q3ではそのヒーローが持つ特殊能力を訪ねます。これをより具体的に書かせることによって，ヒーロー像がよりはっきりとして来ます。ぜひ２文以上書かせるように机間巡視しながら適切なアドバイスを送ってください。

36 Alone on an island

一問一答
3分×9回
まとめ
目安20分

もしも無人島にひとりでいるならば…？

実施おすすめ学年

1年	2年	3年
○	◎	○

使用する文法事項

want to ～，未来表現，接続詞 if など

毎回1つずつ，3分間で質問に答えましょう！

1. You are on an island alone. You can bring only three things. So, what is the first one?
2. Why will you bring it?
3. What is the second one?
4. Why will you bring it?
5. What is the third one?
6. Why will you bring it?
7. If one person can stay with you, who is it?
8. Which do you want to do, to live on the island or to leave it?
9. How will you leave the island?

※未習の文法を含む質問はカットするか，既習文法を用いた同意の質問に作りかえるなどアレンジしてください。

Ⓐ 一問一答の解答例

1. The first one is a knife.
2. Because I have to cut things and fight.
3. The second one is a match box.
4. Because I need fire.
5. The third one is medicine.
6. Because I will get sick.
7. My brother. He is very big and strong.
8. I want to leave it.
9. I will make a boat and go home.

Ⓐ まとめ英作文の例

　I'm on an island and I have only three things. They must be very important and useful things. The first one is a knife because I have to cut things and fight. I will use it to make a lot of things to help me. I can use it to fight too.

　The second one is a match box because I need fire. I will cook food and make light at night. I can use it to be warm when it's cold too.

　The third one is medicine because I will get sick. If it rains, I might catch a cold. It is dangerous to get sick without medicine. Anyway, my brother is with me. He likes sports, so his body is very big and strong. He will help me carry heavy things and fight. We will make a boat and go home together! It will be a very great adventure.

⚠ 指導上の留意点

　無人島にたった一人残されてしまうが，3つだけものを持って行ってよい。あなたなら，何を持っていく？　というテーマです。実在する物品であればなんでも（ついでに言えば，人でもよい）3つだけ持っていくことができます。欲張りな生徒は"many foods""many books"などと書いてしまうのですが，ちょっと待った。3つしか持っていけないので，manyは使えません。また，無人島は当然，圏外です。ケータイ電話，スマホは使用することができません。

　全くヒントがない状態で書かせた方が，面白いものを持っていく生徒が出て来たりして楽しいのですが，10個程度のアイテムをこちらからあらかじめ提示して，その中から3つ選んで持っていくというルールにしても構いません。（こちらの方が，発想力が必要ないので簡単に書かせることができます）

　文法的には，未来のwillを使う程度で，とても平易な文法しか使用しません。それでいてテーマとしてとても面白いものになっていますので，1年生から3年生まで，どの学年にでも楽しめるテーマだと思います。

➕1 センテンス

　Q2・4・6では，どのように使う？（How will you use it?）のような質問を付け加えると，より具体的に書いてくれることでしょう。

37 Win the lottery

一問一答
3分×7回
まとめ
目安20分

もしも宝くじがあたったら…？

実施おすすめ学年

1年	2年	3年
	◎	○

使用する文法事項

want to ～，have to ～，接続詞 if, feel c,
How much ～
など

毎回１つずつ，３分間で質問に答えましょう！

1. How do you feel if you win the lottery?
2. How much money will you get?
3. Will you tell anyone about it? Why?
4. You have to use all the money. So, what will you buy/do?
5. Why will you buy/do it?
6. What will happen then?
7. If you can buy/do one more thing, what is it?

※未習の文法を含む質問はカットするか，既習文法を用いた同意の質問に作りかえるなどアレンジしてください。

A 一問一答の解答例

1. I will be shocked and very happy!
2. 100,000,000 yen.
3. No, I won't. Because people will get my money.
4. I will not work. I will only travel every day.
5. I want to see the world.
6. I will become the happiest person.
7. I will help other people.

A まとめ英作文の例

If I win 100,000,000 yen, I will be shocked and very happy! At first, I will not believe it. But I will punch myself and I will believe it then! Because it is a lot of money. I will say, "Unbelievable!" But I won't tell people about it because they will get my money. My family and friends will try to get my money. It will be my super-secret. After that, I will not work anymore. I will live peacefully at a big house.

I want to travel every day because I want to see the world. I want to visit all of the countries. Also, I will eat the food in every country. If I can, I will use my money and help other people too. Especially the people in poor countries.

Then, I will become the happiest person. Money is happiness! I want to win a lot of money!

⚠ 指導上の留意点

これは，もし宝くじが当たったら，何をする？　というトピックです。誰もが宝くじが当たった時のことは想像すると思います。それは中学生でも同じで，突然手に入れた大金で，何を買うでしょう，または，何をするでしょう。想像の世界なので，なんでもできるというのがこのトピックのよいところです。中学生ならではの豊かな想像力で，楽しい英文を書かせましょう。

宝くじが当たったらどんな気分になるでしょう（Q1）。当たったことを人に伝えるかどうかは悩むところですね（Q3）。全額使わなければならないとしたら（貯金は不可），何をしましょうか？（Q4）筆者だったら，豪邸を建てて，高級車を買います。教師の仕事は続けるかなぁ。

文法的には want to や will を使う機会が多くなりますので2年生向きのトピックと言えますが，もちろん3年生にも有効ですし，will や want to を使わないで，動詞の現在形を使っても書かせることができますので，1年生にも楽しんでもらえるトピックだと思います。

➕1 センテンス

Q4・5のところを，何を買う（する）だけでなく，それからのストーリーをプラスワンで書かせましょう。3分で書き足らない時は，後日「まとめ」の時間でじっくり書けばよいと伝えてあげましょう。

38 If you are a teacher…

もしもあなたが先生になったら…？

実施おすすめ学年

1年	2年	3年
	◎	○

使用する文法事項

want to ～，have to ～，接続詞 if など

毎回1つずつ，3分間で質問に答えましょう！

1. What subject do you want to teach?
2. Why do you want to teach the subject?
3. What club do you want to do?
4. Why do you want to do the club?
5. Which year do you want to teach?
6. Why do you want to teach them?
7. What kind of students do you want to teach?
8. What is needed to be a good teacher?
9. In your school now, who do you think is a good teacher?
10. Why do you think so?

※未習の文法を含む質問はカットするか，既習文法を用いた同意の質問に作りかえるなどアレンジしてください。

A 一問一答の解答例

1. I want to teach computer.
2. Computers are really important in our lives today.
3. I want to do the computer club too.
4. Because I want students to learn how to use a computer.
5. I want to teach the first grade in junior high school.
6. Because they are fun and exciting.
7. I want to teach students who are happy.
8. Knowledge is needed.
9. I think our homeroom teacher is a good example.
10. Because we like our homeroom teacher!

A まとめ英作文の例

　I want to teach computer. Computers are really important in our lives today. It is used everywhere. It helps us and makes our lives easier.

　I want to do the computer club too, because I want students to learn how to use a computer.

　I want to teach the first grade in junior high school, because they are fun and exciting students. I want to teach students who are happy. Because happy students will learn faster.

　Knowledge and understanding are needed to be a good teacher. I think our homeroom teacher is a good example, because we all like our homeroom teacher! I want to be like him some day!

⚠ 指導上の留意点

　もしあなたが先生だったら，何を教えますか？　というテーマです。

　中学生は，いつもは生徒として何かを教わる立場ですが，このテーマでは先生になって，何を教えるのか，部活動は何を見たいのか，何年生を教えたいのか，といった質問に答えていきます。

　生徒全員が将来の夢として教師になりたいと思っているわけではありませんが，もし自分が教師だったらどんな教師になりたいかというテーマには，生徒は案外食いついてきます。生徒にとって書いていて楽しいテーマの一つです。

　Q7では自分にとってよい生徒とは？　という質問をしていますが，これに対する答えは，生徒の深層心理では，生徒自身がそうなりたいと思っている目標の生徒像なのかもしれません。

　Q9，Q10では実際の学校の先生を挙げさせていますが，書かせることが難しいのであれば，カットしてしまっても構いません。その代わりに新たに質問を付け加えることも，もちろん構いません。

➕1 センテンス

　Q7やQ8では，その理由を書かせてみるとよりよい作文になっていくと思います。

39 My final day

一問一答
3分×8回
まとめ
目安20分

地球最後の日

実施おすすめ学年

1年	2年	3年
	◎	○

使用する文法事項

want to 〜，未来表現
など

毎回1つずつ，3分間で質問に答えましょう！

1. Today is the last day of the world. What will you do in the morning?
2. Why will you do it?
3. After that, what will you do in the afternoon?
4. Why will you do it?
5. Then, what will you do at night?
6. Why will you do it?
7. On the last one hour, what will you do?
8. What will you say to your family?

※未習の文法を含む質問はカットするか，既習文法を用いた同意の質問に作りかえるなどアレンジしてください。

Ⓐ 一問一答の解答例

1. I will wake up early and have a big breakfast.
2. Because I want to see the sun in the morning.
3. I will go to Disneyland.
4. Because it is the happiest place on Earth.
5. I will see some stars.
6. Because they are very beautiful.
7. I will laugh and laugh.
8. I will say thank you and I love you.

Ⓐ まとめ英作文の例

On the last day of the world, I will wake up early because I want to see the sun in the morning. Watching it makes me really happy. I will have a very big breakfast. I will eat fried egg, pancakes, sausages, and bread with butter. I will drink a lot of coffee to get energy.

Then I will go to Disneyland because it is the happiest place on Earth. I will buy many things and eat a lot of Disney food. I want to eat the special Disney dishes. I will try all of the interesting rides there.

At night, I will see some stars and the moon because they are very beautiful. I will not sleep. At last, I will laugh and laugh. After that, I think I will cry. But I will be happy. And I will say thank you and I love you to my family.

⚠ 指導上の留意点

「もし，今日が地球最後の日だったら…？」というテーマです。Q1「まず，朝に何をする？」What will you do in the morning? に始まり，Q3「午後には何をする？」What will you do in the afternoon? Q5「夜には何をする？」What will you do at night? 最後は，Q7「最後の1時間は何をする？」On the last one hour, what will you do? で締めます。

以上のように，このテーマでは助動詞 will を用いた未来表現を何回も使用しますので，2年生に最も適しているテーマだと思います。頭の中で「地球最後の日」を想像しながら，自分の行動を will を使って表現していくのです。もちろん架空の話ですから，そこに発想力や想像力が必要になってきます。そうしたタスクが表現の能力を育んでいくのです。

人それぞれの「地球最後の日」ですから，「鑑賞会」ではとても意欲的にクラスメイトの作品を鑑賞しようとします。感心させられたり，笑わせられたり，驚かされたり，クラスメイトの作品がとてもよい「読み物」になるのです。「3分英作文」で「鑑賞会」まできちんとやれば，ライティングの力だけでなく，リーディングの力までついて来るのです。

➕1 センテンス

Q2・4・6では，より具体的な記述にさせるために，机間巡視をしながら適宜 "Where?" "What?" などをつぶやいてあげるとよいでしょう。

40 100 years in the future

一問一答
3分×9回
まとめ
目安20分

100年後の世界はどんなだろう？

実施おすすめ学年

1年	2年	3年
	◎	○

使用する文法事項

未来表現，I think ～，接続詞 if，want to ～
など

毎回1つずつ，3分間で質問に答えましょう！

1. Do you think the world will be a better place then?
2. Give some examples of future technology. (3-5 things)
3. What will happen to the world?
4. What will happen to your country?
5. What will happen to your family?
6. Do you want to live in that time?
7. If you are living there, what will you do then?
8. If you can bring one future technology here, what is it?
9. Why did you choose it?

※未習の文法を含む質問はカットするか，既習文法を用いた同意の質問に作りかえるなどアレンジしてください。

Ⓐ 一問一答の解答例

1. I think it will be a little bit better.
2. There will be flying cars, super smart computers, very strong and healthy people, and we don't use paper money anymore.
3. The world will be really scary.
4. Japan will be full of robots and machines.
5. My children will have super children!
6. Yes, I do.
7. I will see everything and try them all.
8. The super medicine.
9. Because it can help a lot of people.

Ⓐ まとめ英作文の例

A hundred years in the future, I think it will be a little bit better. There will be a lot of wonderful machines. There will be flying cars, super smart computers, very strong and healthy people, and we don't use paper money anymore.

I think there will be a lot of changes. The world will be really scary. But it will be wonderful too. Japan will be full of robots and machines. Everything is quick and convenient.

I think my children will be amazing and have super children! They will be smart, strong, and beautiful or handsome.

I want to live there, because I want to see everything and try them all. If I can bring one thing from the future, I want to bring the super medicine back here because it can help a lot of people.

⚠ 指導上の留意点

100年後の世界はどうなっているだろう？　という想像を膨らませるトピックです。AIの発達などで現在においてもどんどん世界は便利になっています。そのさらに100年後の世界を想像させてみましょう。

私は高校生時代，ポケベルを使って一生懸命数字の「当て字」で「＊２＊２」と押してからコミュニケーションを取っていたので，まさかスマートフォンのようなものがそのたった10数年後に現れるとは思ってもいませんでした。

よく，今までに人間が未来像として想像してきたものは，ほとんどのものが実現してきていると言われています。ここで生徒が想像して書いたものが実現したら，とても面白いですね。

文法的には，未来のことですので，willを用いる文が多くなります。その意味ではこのトピックは２年生に向いているかもしれません。また，作文というとどうしてもIで始まる文ばかり書いてしまう（私は「アイアイ作文」と呼んでいる）のですが，このトピックではいろんな主語で英文を書かせることができるかと思います。

➕1 センテンス

Q2では，具体的にどんな機能が備わっているのか，どんな新しいものが生まれているのかをどんどん書かせましょう。

41 A person from the past

一問一答
3分×9回
まとめ
目安20分

歴史上の偉人がやってくるヤァ！ヤァ！ヤァ！

実施おすすめ学年

1年	2年	3年
	◎	○

使用する文法事項

過去形，接続詞 if，未来表現，I think 〜 など

毎回1つずつ，3分間で質問に答えましょう！

1. Who is your favorite historical person?
2. Where/what time was the person from?
3. What did the person do?
4. Why do you like him/her?
5. If he/she is here now, what will he/she feel?
6. What will be the most surprising thing for him/her?
7. What will he/she say about current events?
8. Do you think he/she will like it here?
9. What will you say to him/her?

※未習の文法を含む質問はカットするか，既習文法を用いた同意の質問に作りかえるなどアレンジしてください。

A 一問一答の解答例

1. Albert Einstein.
2. He was from Germany about 100 years ago.
3. He was a genius who helped the world.
4. Because he was a smart and great man.
5. He will feel surprised. He will be shocked.
6. The smartphone and the Internet.
7. He will feel sad because the world is not peaceful.
8. Yes, he will. He liked technology.
9. Thank you and sorry!

A まとめ英作文の例

My favorite historical person is Albert Einstein. He is very famous now. He was a scientist. He was from Germany about one hundred years ago. It was a time during the war. He was a genius who helped the world. He developed many useful things. They are things that are still useful today. I like him because he was a smart man. I want to be smart like him.

If he is here now, he will be surprised. He will be shocked at the smartphone. He will be very shocked at the Internet. But he will feel sad because the world is not peaceful. There are many problems everywhere. But I think he will like it here because he liked technology.

He will love the computer. I will say thank you and sorry to him.

⚠ 指導上の留意点

もしも過去から歴史上の人物が現在にやってきたら…というテーマです。

歴史上の人物が現在にやってきたら，どんな気持ちになるでしょうか。きっと驚くことでしょうね。

電話を発明したとされるグラハム・ベルが現在にやってきてスマートフォンを見たら，どんな気持ちになるでしょう。ガリレオ・ガリレイが現在にやってきて宇宙船に乗り，宇宙から地球を見たらどんな気持ちになるでしょう。あるいは，沢村栄一が現在にやってきてプロ野球チームに入団したら，何勝できるでしょうか。

このように，このテーマでは，実際に歴史上の人物を一人選んで，その人物が現在にやってきたらどんなことを感じ，どんなことを言うのかを想像し，英作文していくのです。

その人物は現在の状況を気に入ってくれるでしょうか。気に入ってくれるといいですけど，そうではないかもしれません。そんなこともその人物になったつもりで心情を考えて，英作文するのです。

➕1 センテンス

Q8は，続けて Why? と尋ねてみることで，なぜ現在を気に入った（気に入らなかった）のかの理由を，プラスワンセンテンスとして引き出すことができます。

42 The final meal

一問一答
3分×7回
まとめ
目安20分

最後の晩餐

実施おすすめ学年

1年	2年	3年
○	◎	○

使用する文法事項

未来表現，接続詞 if，want to ～
など

毎回1つずつ，3分間で質問に答えましょう！

1. If you can eat one last time, what do you want to eat?
2. Why did you choose it?
3. Do you want to eat anything else?
4. Who do you want to eat it with?
5. Where do you want to eat it?
6. How do you feel when you eat it?
7. What will you say after?

※未習の文法を含む質問はカットするか，既習文法を用いた同意の質問に作りかえるなどアレンジしてください。

Ⓐ 一問一答の解答例

1. I want to eat a whole pizza.
2. Because pizza is my favorite food.
3. Also, I want to eat fried chicken.
4. I want to eat it with my best friend.
5. At a beautiful restaurant near the beach.
6. I feel happy but sad.
7. "This is the best!"

Ⓐ まとめ英作文の例

　I want to eat a whole pizza as my last meal because pizza is my favorite food. I usually have pizza on my birthday. It is a special dish for me. I want pizza that has a lot of meat, vegetables, and cheese. I like cheese very much. Eating food with cheese makes me very happy.

　Also, I want to eat fried chicken. My favorite chicken is the one from KFC. It is very delicious but really expensive. I don't eat it often.

　I want to eat it with my best friend at a beautiful restaurant near the beach. There will be music and a lot of delicious drinks. We will talk about many memories. We will look at pictures and videos. It will be great. We will have a good time together.

　I think I will feel happy and sad. But I will not cry. Then I will say, "This is the best!"

⚠ 指導上の留意点

　不治の病に冒された，天変地異が起こった，などの理由で，これが最後の食事になりそう。さて，あなたならば，何を最後の食事に選びますか？　というテーマです。

　いわゆる「最後の晩餐」と呼ばれるものです。まだ若く，人生これからの中学生にはあまりイメージがわかないかもしれませんが，テーマとしてはとても面白いものになります。

　「好きな食べ物」というのは英作文のテーマとしては一般的ですが，それではありきたりです。やはり少しひねったテーマの方が生徒も熱心に書くというものです。

　そもそも，好きな食べ物が「最後の晩餐」になるとは限りません。筆者はラーメンが大好きで，一時期，年間300杯以上を食べるラーメンフリークでしたが，だからと言ってラーメンを「最後の晩餐」にしようとは思いません。やはり，最後は母親が作ったカレーが食べたいなあと思っています。

　生徒たちも「最後の晩餐」にはとても頭を悩ませていました。給食のカレー，座布団のように大きなステーキ，おかゆ，チョコレートなどなど，生徒は思い思いに自分の「最後の晩餐」をチョイスし，黙々と英作文をしていきますよ。

➕1 センテンス

　Q2「なぜその食べ物を選ぶのか」という質問がこのテーマの大切なところです。ぜひ，why? だけではなく効果的な質問を付け足してプラスワン書かせてみましょう。

Chapter 2　表現力大幅アップ！3分英作文　おすすめテーマ

43 The perfect world

一問一答
3分×9回
まとめ
目安20分

理想の世界

実施おすすめ学年

1年	2年	3年
	◎	○

使用する文法事項

want to 〜, have to 〜, 接続詞 if
How long 〜, How much 〜,
make O C
など

毎回1つずつ，3分間で質問に答えましょう！

1. What is the name of your perfect world?
2. How big is it?
3. How much water and land does it have?
4. How long is one day there?
5. What are its seasons?
6. Give examples of its plants and animals.
7. Are there people on it?
8. What makes that world special? (3-5 reasons)
9. Do you want to live in that world?

※未習の文法を含む質問はカットするか，既習文法を用いた同意の質問に作りかえるなどアレンジしてください。

Ⓐ 一問一答の解答例

1. Paradise.
2. It is bigger than Earth.
3. Half is water and half is land.
4. There are 30 hours in one day.
5. It has a cool summer and a warm winter.
6. There are delicious vegetables and fruits. The animals are nice and very friendly.
7. Yes, there are people.
8. People can fly there. Also, there is magic. It is a very convenient and exciting place. Everyone is happy, so no one does bad things.
9. Yes, I do.

Ⓐ まとめ英作文の例

My world is called "Paradise" and it is bigger than the Earth. Half of the world is water and half is land. But the countries are much bigger and the oceans are much wider. There are 30 hours in one day. We can do more things in one day there.

It has a cool summer and a warm winter. Every day is comfortable. There are a lot of delicious vegetables and fruits. The animals are nice and very friendly. They are good pets and smart too. People there can fly. Also, there is magic. You can do a lot of amazing things! It is a very convenient and exciting place. Everyone is happy, so no one does bad things. I want to live there. It is my perfect world.

⚠ 指導上の留意点

もし，地球外に理想の世界があったら，それはどんな世界だろう。このテーマでは，そんな「理想郷」を書かせます。

人それぞれ，自分の理想の世界（星）像は異なると思います。植物が好きな人にとっての理想は，やはり美しい植物が生い茂った世界なのでしょうし，筆者は犬が大好きなので，私以外は全部犬，なんていう世界（星）がもしあれば，幸せなことこの上ないです。（猿の惑星ならぬ，犬の惑星？）生徒はこのテーマで，SF映画の作者になったような気分で，どんどん書き進めていくと思います。

文法的にはhow big，how much，さらにhow longといったhowを用いた質問が続きますので，生徒がある程度疑問文を理解した段階でこのテーマを採用した方が効果的かと思います。Q8は What makes that world special? といわゆる「make O C」の文を用いていますが，これがもし難しいようであれば，What is the special points of that world? でも構いません。（何度でも書きますが，生徒の実態に応じていくらでもアレンジできるのが「3分英作文」のよいところなんです）

➕1 センテンス

Q8では3〜5つの理由を書かせます。時間的に余裕がないようであれば，3回に分けて（3分×3回）行っても構いません。

44 The perfect school

一問一答
3分×9回
まとめ
目安20分

理想の学校

実施おすすめ学年

1年	2年	3年
	◎	○

使用する文法事項

want to 〜, have to 〜, 助動詞 can, make O C
など

毎回1つずつ，3分間で質問に答えましょう！

1. What is the name of your perfect school?
2. Where is it?
3. How big is it?
4. Give examples of its school rules. (3-5 rules)
5. What subjects can you study there?
6. What is your school's slogan?
7. What do the uniforms look like?
8. What makes the school special?
9. Do you want to study at that school?

※未習の文法を含む質問はカットするか，既習文法を用いた同意の質問に作りかえるなどアレンジしてください。

Ⓐ 一問一答の解答例

1. Very High School.
2. It is near Disneyland.
3. It is very big.
4. You must talk in a very big voice. You must speak English very well. You must run very fast. You must study very hard. You must be very beautiful.
5. You can study all subjects.
6. The slogan is, "Be the very best."
7. They look very cool and expensive.
8. It is special because everyone is very good at everything.
9. No, I don't.

Ⓐ まとめ英作文の例

　Very High School is near Disneyland. It has its own train station. It is a very big high school. It has a large park and two lakes. Students <u>must talk in a very big voice</u>, <u>speak English very well</u>, <u>run very fast</u>, <u>study very hard, and be very beautiful</u>. Everyone is perfect.

　<u>You can study all subjects</u> there. PE, math, English, Japanese, and other languages too. They are not difficult.

　<u>The slogan is, "We are the very best."</u> The uniforms <u>look very cool and expensive</u> too. They were designed by a famous fashion designer from France.

　<u>The school is special because everyone is very good at everything.</u> But <u>I don't want to go there.</u> I will go to a normal high school.

⚠ 指導上の留意点

　自分にとって理想の学校とは、どんな学校でしょうか。理想の学校を設立してみましょう、というのがこのテーマです。

　理想の学校は生徒によって様々だと思います。運動が好きな生徒にとっての理想の学校は、毎日1時間目から6時間目までずっと体育の授業しかないような学校でしょうし、英語が好きな生徒にとっては、どんな授業も英語で教えてくれる学校が理想の学校でしょう。

　まずは学校名から（Q1）始まり、どこにあるのか（Q2）、どんな校則があるのか（Q4）、校訓は何か（Q6）、といった質問に毎回次々と答えていくだけで、自分にとっての理想の学校ができ上がります。

　もちろん実際に存在するわけではありませんので、どんな学校でも構わないわけです。自分が学校の設立者になった気分で、自分の理想の学校を、想像力を働かせて作っていくのです。

　最後に行う「鑑賞会」で、クラスメイトの作品を鑑賞しあって、最後に自分が入学したい学校に投票して、クラス1・学年1の人気校を決定してみたらいかがでしょう。

➕1 センテンス

　Q4は3分以内で書かせるには少し負荷が高いと思うのであれば、3～5回に分けて書かせてみてもいいと思います。もちろん、1回だけで書かせ、続きは「まとめ」の時間に、というやり方でも構いません。

Interview with a celebrity

セレブに突撃インタビュー！

実施おすすめ学年

1年	2年	3年
○	◎	○

使用する文法事項

want to ～，接続詞 if，
3人称単数現在，未来表現
など

毎回1つずつ，3分間で質問に答えましょう！

1. Who is your favorite celebrity?
2. How old is he/she?
3. Where does he/she live?
4. What does he/she do?
5. Why is he/she your favorite?
6. What will you say if you meet him/her?
7. If you can ask him/her some questions, what will you ask?
8. Do you want to be his/her friend?
9. Do you want to live like him/her?

※未習の文法を含む質問はカットするか，既習文法を用いた同意の質問に作りかえるなどアレンジしてください。

A 一問一答の解答例

1. My favorite is Justin Bieber.
2. He is older than me.
3. He lives in America.
4. He is a singer.
5. Because he has a great voice and he looks cool.
6. I will say, "I am your greatest fan!"
7. I will ask him, "Is it difficult to be famous?"
8. Yes, I want to be his friend.
9. No, I don't want to be like him.

A まとめ英作文の例

　My favorite celebrity is Justin Bieber. He is a handsome boy and he is very famous. He is known all over the world. He is older than me and he lives in America. His songs are really popular there and around the world. His songs make people want to dance. I like listening to all of them.

　He is a singer, he has a great voice, and he looks cool too. So, he has a lot of fans. I'm one of his fans. I'm a big fan! If I meet him, I will say to him, "I am your greatest fan!" I want to get his sign.

　Then, I will ask him, "Is it difficult to be famous?" I think it is difficult to be famous like him. So, I want to be his friend but I don't want to be like him. I will be his greatest fan forever.

⚠ 指導上の留意点

　有名人にインタビューをしてみましょう，というのがこのテーマです。中学生にとって憧れの有名人を一人選んで，その有名人に様々な質問をしていきます。

　まずは，その有名人のプロフィールを書いていきます。名前（Q1），住んでいるところ（Q2），職業（Q3）がそれに該当します。続いて，なぜその人物が有名なのかを書きます（Q5）。歌手であれば，有名な歌があったり，俳優であれば，その人を有名にした映画やドラマがあったりするはずですね。

　次に，実際にその有名人と会話をします。最初に何を言うか（Q6），次に，いくつか質問をしていきます（Q7）。

　Q8では，その有名人と友達になりたいかどうかを生徒に質問します。最後にQ9で，その有名人のようになりたいかどうかを質問します。

　文法的には，別段難しい文法を使っておりませんので，1年生からでも十分に指導可能なテーマです。ただ，有名人という第三者を扱いますので，三人称を学習している必要はあります。

➕1 センテンス

　Q7では有名人に聞いてみたい質問を考えさせますが，2つ以上は考えさせてみたいですね。

　Q8では，なぜ友達になりたい（なりたくない）のかを，プラスワンとして書かせるといいでしょう。

46 Three new school rules

一問一答　3分×9回　まとめ　目安20分

3つの新しい校則

実施おすすめ学年

1年	2年	3年
	◎	○

使用する文法事項

未来表現，接続詞 if
など

毎回1つずつ，3分間で質問に答えましょう！

1. What is a school rule that you do not like?
2. Why don't you like it?
3. If you make three new school rules, what is the first one?
4. Why is that a good rule?
5. What is the second one?
6. Why is that a good rule?
7. What is the third one?
8. Why is that a good rule?
9. What will happen if they are real rules?

※未習の文法を含む質問はカットするか，既習文法を用いた同意の質問に作りかえるなどアレンジしてください。

A 一問一答の解答例

1. You have to wear a uniform in school.
2. I want to wear comfortable clothes.
3. You can use smartphones at school.
4. Because smartphones are very useful for everything!
5. You can wear anything.
6. Because it will make students happy.
7. You can wear warmer clothes during winter at school.
8. Because it is very cold during winter.
9. The school will become a very happy place.

A まとめ英作文の例

　There are many rules in school. I have to follow all the rules every time. It is difficult sometimes. For example, you have to wear a uniform in school. The uniform is not comfortable to me. It makes me tired. I want to wear comfortable clothes.

　I have three new rules. The first rule is "You can use smartphones at school". It will help us because smartphones are very useful for everything!

　The second rule is "You can wear anything". It's a good rule because it will make students happy. Happy students can study better.

　The third rule is "You can wear warmer clothes during winter at school". It is a useful rule because it is very cold during winter.

　If these three rules are real, the school will become a very happy place. A happy school is the best!

⚠ 指導上の留意点

　もし，こんな校則があったらいいな，という新しい校則を考えるテーマです。

　中学生にとって，こんな校則があったらもっと過ごしやすいのに，というものはあると思います。それを中学生の自由な発想で，英語で書いてもらうのです。

　最も，そういう学校が本当にあったらとんでもないことになりそうですが（笑），そういうとんでもないことを考えさせるところが，中学生の「書いてみたい」という意欲を刺激するのです。本書には51のテーマを掲載していますが，このテーマは非常に人気のあったテーマの一つです。

　一番多いのは「スマホ・ゲームを持ってきてもよい」というものです。「服装は自由」「朝食も給食で出る」なども多いでしょうか。生徒はそう思っているんだ，ということがこちらもわかって面白いです。

　文法的には，can（この場合は「〜できる」というよりは「〜してもよい」の意味に近いと思いますが）を使用する場面が多いと思います。「〜しなければならない」のhave to も使う場面があると思います。そういった助動詞を定着させるためには有効なテーマだと思います。

➕1 センテンス

　プラスワンというより，ここではQ9までで3つの校則を書いてもらっていますが，「まとめ」の時間でどんどん4つ目，5つ目を書いてもらいましょう。

Chapter 2　表現力大幅アップ！3分英作文　おすすめテーマ　115

47 Planning a school trip

楽しい修学旅行計画

実施おすすめ学年

1年	2年	3年
	◎	○

使用する文法事項

未来表現，接続詞 if，How long ～ など

毎回1つずつ，3分間で質問に答えましょう！

1. If you plan a school trip, where will you go?
2. Why will you go there?
3. What places can you visit there?
4. What are its famous dishes?
5. What will you do there?
6. How will you go there?
7. Where will you stay?
8. How long is the trip?

※未習の文法を含む質問はカットするか，既習文法を用いた同意の質問に作りかえるなどアレンジしてください。

A 一問一答の解答例

1. I will go to Okinawa.
2. Because it is very beautiful there.
3. There are a lot of beautiful beaches and castles.
4. Murasaki imo and sata andagi.
5. I will swim in the sea with my friends.
6. I will go by plane.
7. I will stay at a hotel near the beach.
8. A week.

A まとめ英作文の例

　I really liked our school trip. If I plan my school trip, I will go to Okinawa. It is at the south of Japan. It is a very famous place. Many people visit Okinawa every year. I have never been there but I want to go because it is very beautiful there. There are a lot of beautiful beaches and a lot of old castles. They are always in posters. Okinawa is also famous for murasaki imo. It is a purple sweet potato. Sata andagi is also famous. It is fried bread like agepan. I will eat them and I will buy some for my family. I want to swim in the sea with my friends. We will have a lot of fun!

　I will go there by plane. I want to stay at a hotel near the beach for a week. It will be a great memory for me.

⚠ 指導上の留意点

　このテーマは，自分が教師になった気分で，校外学習を企画してみましょう，というテーマです。

　「行ってみたい場所」「行ってみたい国」というのはごく一般的な英作文のテーマだと思います。要は，結局のところこのテーマは，その「行ってみたい場所」と書く内容がほぼ同じになるのですが，単に「行ってみたい場所を書きましょう」という課題を与えるよりは「教師になったつもりで，校外学習を企画してみましょう」とやった方が，盛り上がり方が変わってきます。

　何事も，より興味を持って意欲的にやってもらった方がよいのです。こうしたちょっとした工夫をするだけで，生徒は食いついてきます。「3分英作文」は，生徒が（教師も）負担と感じている英作文を，少しでも負担を減らし，少しでも興味を持って意欲的に取り組んでもらいたいという筆者の思いがあって取り組ませてきたものです。

　このテーマの他にも「結局このテーマって，あれと同じじゃないか」というテーマが本書にはありますが，直球勝負に飽きた生徒に対してたまには変化球でも，と思っている時に使ってください。

➕1 センテンス

　Q3やQ4では有名なスポットや食べ物を挙げさせています。そのスポットや食べ物について，プラスワンで詳しく書くように伝えてみましょう。

48 What is the most important for you to do?

一問一答
3分×8回
まとめ
目安20分

コレをするのは超大切です

実施おすすめ学年

1年	2年	3年
		◎

使用する文法事項
不定詞（It is 〜 for 〜 to do），接続詞 if
want 人 to 〜，未来表現
など

毎回1つずつ，3分間で質問に答えましょう！

1. What is important for you to do?
2. When/where/how do you do it?
3. Why is it important?
4. Is it difficult for you to do?
5. If you don't do it, what will happen?
6. If you do it every day, what will happen?
7. Do you want others to do it too?
8. If everyone does it too, what will happen?

※未習の文法を含む質問はカットするか，既習文法を用いた同意の質問に作りかえるなどアレンジしてください。

A 一問一答の解答例

1. It is important for me to study English.
2. I study English at school and at home every day.
3. Because it is used all over the world.
4. Yes, it is.
5. I won't learn English well.
6. I'll be very good at English.
7. Yes, I do.
8. Everyone can communicate with one another.

A まとめ英作文の例

　It is important for me to study English. I study English at school every day. Sometimes, I study English at home too. I study it <u>because it is used all over the world</u>. But it is difficult for me to study English. There are a lot of words and rules!

　Also, I don't want to study for a long time. Studying makes me very tired. But if I don't study, <u>I won't learn it well</u>. If I don't learn it, I won't speak it well. So I will study English more to become very good at it.

　Then I can speak to foreigners who speak English. I think it is better if people learn English. Also, we must use it often and speak English. Then, <u>everyone can communicate with one another</u>. We will understand each other. I think the world will be better.

⚠ 指導上の留意点

「大切なもの」the most important thing つまり「宝物」my treasure はすでに扱いました。(p.30) ここでは「することが大切なもの」the most important thing to do を扱います。

「もの」ではなく「すること」ですから，少しばかりニュアンスが変わってきます。3年生にもなると少し考え方がオトナになってきて，将来に対する思いや，今の自分に足りないものなど，そういったものを踏まえて「今の私には，これをすることが一番大切だ」ということを黙々と書いてくれます。

3年生で不定詞の応用的な用法として仮主語真主語構文（It is ～ for ～ to do）を学習しますが，それを定着させるためのテーマと考えて良いでしょう。

このテーマは「大切なこと」でやっていますが，important の部分を easy, interesting（あるいは exciting/fun）などに変えるだけで，また違ったテーマになります。仮主語真主語構文（It is ～ for ～ to do）を確実に定着させたいのであれば，違ったテーマで何度もチャレンジさせてみてください。授業では important を扱っておいて，定期テストの作文の問題では easy で書かせるといった使い回しもできます。

➕1 センテンス

Q2で3つの疑問詞（when, where, how）を一気に使っていますが，これをプラスワンとして投げかけてみてもよいでしょう。

49 My Youtube channel

一問一答
3分×8回
まとめ
目安20分

チャンネル登録よろしく！私の動画チャンネル

実施おすすめ学年

1年	2年	3年
		◎

使用する文法事項

How often ～，How many ～
など

毎回1つずつ，3分間で質問に答えましょう！

1. What YouTube videos have you watched?
2. Please make your own channel. What is the name of your channel?
3. What kind of videos do you make?
4. Who watches your videos?
5. How often do you make a video?
6. What is your opening line?
7. Who are the guests on your show?
8. How many people watch your channel?

※未習の文法を含む質問はカットするか，既習文法を用いた同意の質問に作りかえるなどアレンジしてください。

A 一問一答の解答例

1. I have watched gaming videos and funny videos.
2. It is called "YouWatchMe".
3. I make interesting videos about Japan.
4. People who are interested in Japan watch them.
5. I make a video every week.
6. "Konnichi wa, everyone!"
7. Hikakin and Pikotaro.
8. One hundred thousand people.

A まとめ英作文の例

　I watch a lot of YouTube videos when I'm free. I usually watch gaming videos and funny videos. I play games so I am interested in it. I like to watch other players try the games. I can learn from them.

　If I have my own channel, it is called "YouWatchMe". I make interesting videos about Japan. People can learn about Japan with my videos. My videos show different places in Japan that are beautiful and interesting. I also try delicious dishes and snacks. I interview foreigners sometimes too.

　I make a video every week. It makes me busy but it is fun for me. I say "Konnichi wa, everyone!" in my videos.

　I have guests on my show. They are Hikakin and Pikotaro. They are famous Youtubers too. My videos are more famous than theirs. One hundred thousand people watch my channel. So, I am rich!

⚠ 指導上の留意点

　ネット動画には様々な面白い動画があります。ユーチューバーと呼ばれる人がいろんな工夫をしながら、視聴者を楽しませてくれています。

　また、子どもが将来なりたい職業ランキングに「ユーチューバー」というのがランクインしたそうです。それだけインターネット動画に対し、生徒は興味を持っているということです。

　このテーマでは、自分が「ユーチューバー」になったつもりで、どんな動画をアップロードしていくのかを考えて、英作文していきます。

　動画チャンネルの名前を決め、どんな種類の動画を公開するのかというのを考えます。Q4では誰を相手に公開するのかというのを書かせますが、どんなプロジェクトでも、対象となるクライアントについて考えるのはマーケティング戦略においてとても重要です。

　Q5では「決め台詞」を考えますが、ぜひユニークな他にない決め台詞を考えてほしいものです。

➕1 センテンス

　Q3で、実際に作成する動画のコンセプトを書かせます。自分が興味を持っていることや、あるいは、自分の特技などを生かして、詳しく書いてもらいたいところです。How（どうやって？）やWhere（どこで？）のような質問を適宜投げかけてプラスワン、プラスツーと書かせていきましょう。

50 Three years of memories

一問一答
3分×7回
まとめ
目安20分

3年間の思い出ぽろぽろ

実施おすすめ学年

1年	2年	3年
		◎

使用する文法事項
最上級（best），受動態，feel C，
want to ～
など

毎回1つずつ，3分間で質問に答えましょう！

1. What was the best event for you in junior high school?
2. When was it held?
3. Where was it held?
4. Who did you do it with?
5. How did you feel about it?
6. Why was it the best event for you?
7. Do you want to do it again? Why?

※未習の文法を含む質問はカットするか，既習文法を用いた同意の質問に作りかえるなどアレンジしてください。

Ⓐ 一問一答の解答例

1. The English Speech Contest.
2. It was held in October.
3. It was in held at Iruma City Community Center.
4. I went there with my classmates and teachers.
5. I was very nervous but excited and happy.
6. Because I did my best and became the champion!
7. Yes, I do. I want to try harder and help my classmates win too.

Ⓐ まとめ英作文の例

<u>The English Speech Contest</u> was <u>held in October at Iruma City Community Center</u>. It was my best memory.

<u>I went there with my classmates and teachers.</u> There were many students from other schools. The students came from all of the Iruma city's junior high schools. They were very good at English. I thought they were amazing. <u>I was very nervous but excited and happy.</u> I practiced hard for it. My teachers helped me a lot. I practiced every day during my summer vacation. It was difficult, but I worked hard.

It was the best event for me <u>because I did my best and became the champion!</u> I will never forget it.

Next time, <u>I want to try harder and help my classmates win too.</u> We will be great at English and become the champions.

⚠ 指導上の留意点

中学校生活３年間の思い出を振り返り，それを英作文させるためのテーマです。テーマの内容的に，卒業を間近に控えた３年生を相手にこのテーマに取り組ませるのが適しています。

卒業するにあたって３年間の思い出を英語でスピーチさせるというのはやってみたいことのひとつだと思いますが，受験期の３年生に対しては３年間の総復習をしてあげたりしなければならなかったりと案外時間が足りないもので，スピーチをしたくてもなかなかできない，といった先生は多いのではないでしょうか。

そこで，「３分英作文」の手法で，毎回３分だけを使って，３年間の総復習と同時並行でスピーチの準備もしていく，というのはいかがでしょうか。生徒たちは中学校の思い出を堂々とスピーチで語ってくれます。その姿はとても感動的で，その姿を見るのは教師冥利に尽きます。

このテーマと，テーマ "My graduation"（p.124）と組みわせて，大作を作らせるのもいいと思います。

➕1 センテンス

Q6では，なぜその出来事が一番思い出に残っているのかを書きます。ストーリーをできるだけ詳しく書いてもらいましょう。「まとめ」の時間でもどんどん書き進めていってもらいますが，「一問一答」の段階である程度書かせておきましょう。

51 My graduation

一問一答
3分×8回
まとめ
目安20分

卒業～きっと忘れない～

実施おすすめ学年

1年	2年	3年
		◎

使用する文法事項

be going to ～, feel C, I think, want to ～
など

毎回1つずつ，3分間で質問に答えましょう！

1. When are you going to graduate?
2. How do you feel about it? Are you excited, happy, or sad?
3. Why do you feel that?
4. Do you think your friends feel the same?
5. Do you want to meet your classmates again?
6. Do you want to be friends with them forever?
7. Do you want to meet your teachers again?
8. Please leave a message to your classmates.

※未習の文法を含む質問はカットするか，既習文法を用いた同意の質問に作りかえるなどアレンジしてください。

A 一問一答の解答例

1. March 24th.
2. I'm very excited and sad.
3. Because I will go to high school without my friends.
4. I think they feel the same.
5. Yes, I do.
6. Yes, I want to be friends.
7. So-so. It's okay.
8. Let's not forget each other!

A まとめ英作文の例

　I'm a third grade junior high school student. I will graduate on March 24th. It is only a few weeks from now. I'm very excited but sad too, because I will go to high school without my friends. They will go to other schools. Their schools are far away from my school. I think they feel the same.

　I want to meet them again and I want to be friends forever. So, I will meet them often. I have their number and e-mail address. I can talk to them anytime. We will go to many places and go on trips. For example, we will visit famous places in Japan. We will visit other countries too. Our children will become friends someday. We are like a big family.

　If I meet my teachers too, it's okay. I will greet them and say thank you. They were strict but kind.

　Anyway, let's not forget each other! See you soon everyone!

⚠ 指導上の留意点

　中学校を卒業するにあたって，どのような思いを持っているかを英語で書かせるテーマです。

　中学校３年間というのは長いようで短く，しかしその中にも色々な思い出が詰まっています。卒業するにあたってどんな気分でいるかを書かせない手はないと思います。

　卒業するにあたり，どんな気分でいるか？（Q2）そしてそれはなぜか？（Q3）という質問だけでなく，クラスメイトも同じように感じているかどうか（Q4）を尋ねることで，クラスメイトのことを想起させ，より生徒の感情が込もった作文を作らせることができます。

　文法的には全く難しい文法は用いていませんので全学年でも取り組めますが，テーマが卒業を扱っているので，当然，３年生の３学期に行うのが適しています。

　この３分英作文を土台として「まとめ」の時間にどんどん作文させ，それを最後にスピーチをさせると，英語の授業として感動的な「締め」になると思いますよ。ぜひやってみてください。

➕1 センテンス

　Q1～8にはありませんが，中学校生活で最も思い出に残った出来事を書かせる質問をしてもよいでしょう。

What is the best event to you?

おわりに

　「教師の働き方改革」が叫ばれています。確かに教師の勤務が過酷だということは問題です。私だって，ツライよりはラクな方がいい。だけど，効果のことは別にして，始めからラクをすることを最優先させてはいけません。それだけは勘違いしてはいけないと，私は一人の教師として強く思っています。優先させるべきは，ラクかどうかより，効果があるかどうかだと思います。個人的には，効果が上がるものであれば大変なものでもやるしかないのかなと思っています。しかし，だからといって，そのまま改良をせずに大変なままで継続するのもイヤなのです。従来の英作文指導のように，力が伸びるけど大変というものを，なんとか改良してコスパを上げて，こちらの負担を軽減することはできないか。「３分英作文」は私のそういうスタンスから生まれた指導法でもあります。

　言うまでもなく，自由に英文を書かせることがいちばん「書く能力」「表現の能力」の向上につながります。しかしながら自由英作文といっても，それまでに何も指導してこなかったのに，いきなり何かひとつテーマを与え，白紙を配り，「テーマはこれね。テーマに従っていれば好きなように書いていいからね。制限時間は50分。はい，じゃあ作文開始！」とやってみたところで，ほとんどの生徒は１文目を書き始めるまでに相当の時間を使ってしまい，50分ではあまり作文できません。中には，50分間白紙のままで何も書けない生徒もいると思います。それも当然です。こちらが何も筋道を立てていないのに，いきなり書ける方がおかしいのです。

　実は私は，駆け出しの頃はそういう指導をしていました。さらに，そうしたこちらの指導のマズさを棚に上げて机間巡視しながら白紙の生徒を見つけると「なんで白紙なんだ。何か書けるだろう。」と言ってしまい，ますます生徒の意欲を減退させ，そのまま白紙で提出してきた生徒には容赦無く最低点をつけて返却する。きちんと書いてきたら書いてきたで，今度は夜遅くまで添削をする。夜遅くまで身を粉にして添削する自分ってエライと思っていた。今思えば本当にダメな教師でした（今もダメ教師ですが）。あの頃の生徒には謝りたい……。

　そこで，何かきちんと英作文の筋道を生徒に示しながらも，自由度を失わずにどんどん書き進めることができる。さらに欲を言えば，こちらの負担も少ない方がいい。そういう英作文指導法を模索していました。そんな時に，所属校が文部科学省の委嘱「外部専門機関と連携した英語指導力向上への取組」を受け，指導者として東京学芸大学名誉教授の金谷憲先生がいらっしゃいました。私はこれを絶好のチャンスだと思いました。私は英語科主任としての特権（？）を生かして，研究テーマを迷わず英作文指導としました。この「３分英作文」は，そうした経緯で金谷先生のご指導の下，同僚の先生方と２年間の研究を経て完成させたものです。決して，私一人だけの力で完成させたものではありません。この英作文指導法の研究をするにあたりご指導をいただいた金谷憲先生，田邊玲先生，佐竹秀樹先生，共に研究に携わった河合

陽子先生，金子季代先生，一緒に面白いテーマを考えたり英作文モデルの作成を手伝ってくれた Roland Austria 先生，埼玉県および入間地区英語教育研究会の先生方，本当にありがとうございました。皆様のお力添えのお陰で，ようやくこうして1つの「形」になりました。

　この「3分英作文」研究の中間発表を所属校で行ったのが平成26年2月14日。初めてこの指導法を外に発表しました。奇しくも，この日は記録的な豪雪でした。私は女子ソフトテニス部の顧問をずっと務めていますが，あの雪で埼玉県の中学ソフトテニスの聖地「くまがやドーム」の屋根が崩落してしまうというソフトテニス界には衝撃的な出来事がありました。それほどの雪が降っていたにもかかわらず，多くの先生方に来校していただいたことは今でも嬉しく思っています。（先生方には，いまだに「あの大雪を降らせたのは雨男の水谷」「あのあと家に帰れなかった」など言われます。その節は，本当にお世話になりました。）

　それ以来数年が経ちますが，その間，埼玉県内で第12回大野政巳英語教育賞において最優秀賞をいただいたり，第40回関東甲信地区英語教育研究協議会（通称，関ブロ）神奈川大会を始め様々な場面で「3分英作文」を紹介したりする機会にも恵まれました。そうした機会で熱意のある先生方にたくさん出逢えたこと，こうして出版して「3分英作文」を広める機会に恵まれたことも，私にとっては財産です。「3分英作文」が私を育ててくれたと言ってもいいでしょう。（くまがやドームも修復が完了し，再びソフトテニスの聖地として生徒の憧れとなっています。）

　本当に私は運がよく，恵まれた教師だと思います。たまたま委嘱を受けた学校に所属していて，たまたま指導者にご指導いただく機会を得た。そしてたまたまよき同僚に恵まれた。たまたま書いた論文で賞をいただき，たまたまそれを目に留めてくださった方にいろんな場所で発表するよう誘っていただいた。たまたまその噂を聴いた出版社の方に，出版の話をいただいた。豪雪の日にデビューした「3分英作文」が，まさかここまで短期間のうちに育っていくとは思ってもいませんでした。今は，それだけ認めてもらえている指導法なのかなと客観的に思っています。本著を手にしていただいた先生方も，どんどん広めていって欲しいなと思います。

　埼玉県の教員として10年目を終え，これからもがんばっていこう！というこの節目の年に，こうして出版をして自分の指導法を紹介することができたことを大変幸せに思っています。出版のお声がけをいただいた明治図書の広川様に感謝の気持ちを贈ります。

　最後に，この「3分英作文」はまだまだ発展途上の指導法だと思っています。実際にやってみてこういう改良点が見つかった，本著を読んでわからないところがあるから質問したい，新しい英作文テーマを考案した，そして「3分英作文」以外でも私に伝えたいことがもしありましたら，3pun.mizutani@gmail.com までメールを頂ければ幸いです。

平成30年6月　実家の犬，サツキとコウメのことを想いながら。

水谷　大輔

【著者紹介】
水谷　大輔（みずたに　だいすけ）
埼玉県入間市立豊岡中学校教諭。昭和56年東京都生まれ。青山学院大学経済学部卒業。会社員（不動産業）を退職後、日本大学通信教育部に編入し、予備校講師をしながら教員免許を取得。都内私立校講師を経て現職。平成27年度・第12回埼玉県大野政巳英語教育賞最優秀賞受賞。平成28年度・英語教育推進リーダー中央研修参加。女子ソフトテニス部顧問一筋10年。

＜メールアドレス＞
3pun.mizutani@gmail.com

〔本文イラスト〕せのおまいこ

中学校英語サポートBOOKS
帯活動で書く力がぐんぐん伸びる
「3分英作文」の指導アイデア

2018年7月初版第1刷刊	©著　者	水　谷　大　輔
2019年1月初版第2刷刊	発行者	藤　原　光　政
	発行所	明治図書出版株式会社

http://www.meijtosho.co.jp
（企画・校正）広川淳志
〒114-0023　東京都北区滝野川7-46-1
振替00160-5-151318　電話03(5907)6704
ご注文窓口　電話03(5907)6668

＊検印省略　　組版所　藤原印刷株式会社

本書の無断コピーは，著作権・出版権にふれます。ご注意ください。

Printed in Japan　　　　ISBN978-4-13-142629-3

もれなくクーポンがもらえる！読者アンケートはこちらから